My Life is But a Weaving

Rhoda Nakibuka Nsibirwa Kalema
An Autobiography

Moran (E. A.) Publishers Limited
Judda Complex, Prof. Wangari Maathai Road,
P.O. Box 30797 - 00100, Nairobi

With offices and representatives in: Uganda, Rwanda, Tanzania,
Malawi and Zambia

www.moranpublishers.com

ISBN 978 9966 63 342 2

Printed and bound by
English Press Ltd

2024   2023   2022   2021
8   7   6   5   4   3   2   1

Contents

Abbreviations and Acronyms

ACFODE	-	Action for Development
ADA	-	Assistant District Administrator
BOAC	-	British Overseas Airways Corporation
CID	-	Criminal Investigations Department
CHOGM	-	Commonwealth Heads of Government Meeting
CMS	-	Church Missionary Society
CPA	-	Commonwealth Parliamentary Association
CP	-	Conservative Party
DP	-	Democratic Party
EDF	-	European Development Fund
FAWE-U	-	Forum for African Women Educationalists - Uganda
FIDA	-	Federacion Internacional de Abogadas (International Federation of Women Lawyers)
FOWODE	-	Forum for Women in Democracy
ICJ	-	International Commission of Jurists
IMF	-	International Monetary Fund
Isis-WICCE	-	Isis-Women's International Cross-Cultural Exchange
KDA	-	Kiboga Development Association
KICWA	-	Kampala International Christian Women Association
KY	-	Kabaka Yekka
LegCo	-	Legislative Council
LIFE	-	Lay Involvement for Evangelism (Ministry)
LSE	-	London School of Economics
NASA	-	National Security Agency
NCC	-	National Consultative Council
NEC	-	National Executive Committee
NGO	-	Non-Governmental Organisation
NICWA	-	Nairobi International Christian Women's Association
NIV	-	New International Version
NKJV	-	New King James Version
NRA	-	National Resistance Army
NRC	-	National Resistance Council

NRM	-	National Resistance Movement
NSS	-	National Security Service
RC	-	Resistance Council
RPF	-	Rwanda Patriotic Front
SU	-	Scripture Union
SRB	-	State Research Bureau
TASO	-	The AIDS Support Organisation
TPDF	-	Tanzania People's Defence Force
UAUW	-	Uganda Association of University Women
UCB	-	Uganda Commercial Bank
UCW	-	Uganda Council of Women
UMA	-	Uganda Manufacturers Association
UMACIS	-	Uganda Manufacturers Association Consultancy and Information Services
UNESCO	-	United Nations Educational, Scientific and Cultural Organization
UNLA	-	Uganda National Liberation Army
UNLF	-	Uganda National Liberation Front
UPC	-	Uganda People's Congress
UPDF	-	Uganda People's Defence Force
UPM	-	Uganda Patriotic Movement
USSIA	-	Uganda Small Scale Industries Association
UWESO	-	Uganda Women's Effort to Save Orphans
UWHA	-	Uganda Women's Hockey Association
UWONET	-	Uganda Women's Network
WHO	-	World Health Organization
YWCA	-	Young Women's Christian Association

Since my youth, God, you have taught me,
and to this day I declare your marvelous deeds.
Even when I am old and grey,
do not forsake me, my God,
Till I declare your power to my next generation,
Your mighty acts to all who are to come.

Psalm 71:17-18 (NIV)

Dedication

To my Parents
My dear husband, William
Our children and grandchildren
My brothers and sisters
And to those who gave me the inspiration to write
my life's story

Acknowledgements

I could never have put the various threads of my life story together without the encouragement and inspiration of many people. Although I cannot mention them all here, I am very grateful for everyone's love, care and interest in my life.

Among those I owe special gratitude are, first, my parents: my father, Martin Luther Nsibirwa, who believed in education for all his children; and my mother, Veronica Namuddu, as well as my whole family who provided a happy home background upon which my life's foundation was laid.

I thank my many teachers at all levels throughout my school life, at King's College Budo and Edinburgh University. They instilled in me values, knowledge and skills.

I am deeply grateful to my children for their keen interest and help as I wrote my story: William, for sourcing extra information and pictures and for stirring my memory; Veronica Nakibule, for overseeing the content, editing and fact checking as we finalised the book, and for funding its publication; Gladys Nalubowa, for her passionate interest and encouragement.

Peter and Sue Woodsford, friends for over 45 years, persistently demanded that I write my story. Peter typed as I wrote some chapters in his study in Cambridge, United Kingdom, in 2009.

Robert Kibuka, at short notice in 2013, when requested by my daughter Gladys Nalubowa, agreed to work on the third draft of this book. He dug up and added a lot on Buganda's and Uganda's political histories. My late sister Janet Mdoe's records on our father's background have been invaluable.

My special thanks go to Elizabeth Kanyogonya, too. For three years, she used her editing experience and love of books to research and check facts. She did her best to make the book as accurate as possible, filling in the gaps and printing out draft after draft. With extraordinary patience, she sorted out the relevant pictures with me.

I thank Professor Phares Mutibwa for his historian's eye, as well as encouraging and generous comments. Thank you Tom Forrest for critiquing my manuscript. Thank you Muniini Mulera for your very useful comments as we finalised the book.

I am very grateful for the solidarity of the Uganda Women's Network (UWONET), led by its Executive Director, Rita Aciro, through which several women's organisations and individuals responded quickly to my appeal for support towards the publishing costs of this book. Thanks to all UWONET staff members and board, Jackie Asiimwe Mwesige and Wellspring Advisors, MIFUMI, Raising Voices, Deborah K. Serwadda, Jean Kemitare, Helen Twongyeire, Lina Zedriga and Jocelyn Bigirwa.

Special appreciation to Chebet Karago who stepped in and took the book to publication stage, but, sadly, passed away before it was published.

Finally, I am grateful to Moran Publishers for their patience and support in publishing my story.

Foreword

Rhoda Kalema's life is in many ways a microcosm of Africa's development: from a large traditional polygamous family under colonialism, through independence struggles and heady post-independence to tragic oppression and eventually, democracy.

We first met Rhoda at her son, William's, graduation in Cambridge in 1973. We were teachers at Busoga College Mwiri in Uganda in the 1960s and were delighted to find William among the few Ugandan students in Cambridge on our return to the UK. William's father was killed in 1972 when William was in his second year. We developed a strong bond with him and, later, with Rhoda and the rest of the Kalema family, and we have shared many family experiences, sorrows, and joys.

Rhoda's is a remarkable story which we and many others have encouraged her to write. She has persevered with 'The Project', as we called it, with determination against a background of a very busy life. Even in retirement, Jajja is always in demand.

An early draft from a writing stay at our home in Cambridge in 2009 bears the motif '*Gakyali Mabaga*' which translates to (so little done, so much to do) and is the motto of her beloved school, King's College Budo. Finally, the book has emerged – the story of a courageous, dedicated and talented Ugandan with a deep Christian faith.

In the West, politicians rush out their memoirs as soon as they leave office but there are just a few personal accounts written by Africans who have made their mark as politicians and, therefore, Rhoda's account of her political life, spanning many decades, is a valuable contribution to the history of Uganda.

There is so much more to this life story that began in a patrician Ganda family, through colonial times and Uganda's troubles, to achievements as member of parliament and government minister. This history is recorded in a moving, personal way. Rhoda's account of the loss of her husband and subsequent struggles that spurred her decision to join politics is particularly poignant. Her contribution to improving the lives of Ugandan women is exceptional and this record of her work for women's rights makes this book an important historical document.

We have a special memory, from our first return to Uganda in 1990, of Rhoda showing us around the Uganda Women's Effort to Save Orphans (UWESO) project in Kiboga, where they were building a school. Rhoda joined the women who were singing as they passed bricks down the line. She wore a badge that read, "When women stop, everything stops."

Throughout the pages of *My life is But a Weaving*, Rhoda's voice comes through vividly as she tells the story of her life. We are so glad that it is now in your hands to read and we commend it.

Sue and Peter Woodsford
Cambridge
September 2019

Preface

I completed this autobiography at the age of 92 and it is the most honest and authentic account of my life.

When I decided to write my life story, my mind took me back to the paths I have walked and I saw how lovingly my heavenly Father has brought me so far. I have many blessed memories and many not-so-happy ones.

For years, many friends and acquaintances implored me to write a book. After every conversation about my life, however brief, I would be asked, "Have you considered writing a book? I shall buy a copy." I would ponder afterwards, with deep humility, "Perhaps they believe there is something worth recording about my story."

I became aware of the importance of writing from one of my earliest mentors, Katie Kibuka, a pioneer champion of women's rights in Uganda, and a dear friend. "To write what one knows is of great benefit to other people," she often told me. She contributed articles to newspapers from as far back as 1958. In the 1970s, she invited me to a three-day writers' conference at Lweza Conference Centre near Kampala. Sadly, I did not attend, partly due to my family responsibilities. She later told me how beneficial the conference had been for her and, from then on, the idea of writing started to preoccupy my mind.

The older I got, the more extensively I read. I particularly love reading the Bible, spiritual and history books, magazines, and newspapers. Most of all, however, I like biographies and autobiographies, most of which have inspired me greatly. I have come face-to-face with several amazing lives and among them are St Alban, the first Christian who was martyred in

England in AD 250; Bishop Polycarp of Smyrna in modern-day Turkey who was born in AD 69 and is among the earliest Christians whose writings have survived; John Wycliffe of Yorkshire, England, who was born in 1330 and was reknowned for translating the scriptures from Latin to English; Martin Luther, the father of Protestant Reformation who was born in 1483 in Germany; Corrie ten Boom (1892-1983), a Christian Dutchwoman whose family helped many Jews escape the Nazi Holocaust during World War II; American missionary and author, Elisabeth Elliot (1926-2015); Sir Apolo Kagwa (1864-1927), the long-serving Katikiro (Prime Minister) of Buganda; Julius Nyerere, the founding father of the United Republic of Tanzania (1922-1999); and Nelson Mandela (1918-2013), the anti-apartheid leader and first African President of South Africa.

Their inspiring stories have convinced me that more people need to write their life stories, for the benefit of the current and future generations. I have often lamented that many invaluable unwritten life experiences are buried with their owners, thus depriving current and future would-be readers, of knowledge on how life can be lived and survived.

I have a habit of jotting down notes in notebooks and on bits of paper whenever I listen to a talk, sermon or read a book. I often come across these notes years later when going through my documents, as happened in 2002. I was invited to present a paper at the 8th International Interdisciplinary Congress on Women: Women's Worlds 2002, at Makerere University. The congress is held every three years and was being hosted in Africa for the first time. As I dug through my papers for information on my topic, 'The Struggle of Women's Emancipation in Uganda, 1914 – 2002', I came across old notes that inspired me to start writing this book.

At the congress, I recall learning something important during the 'How to write for others to read' session. The presenter was clear about one thing: when writing, the truth is very important because it will capture the reader's interest – so no matter how challenging or painful the story may be, it must be told truthfully.

In 2004, Martin Lwanga, the publisher of the *Christian Post magazine*, requested an interview as we walked out of a shopping centre. This also gave me the impetus to search for material about my life. The interview brought out a lot of information about my background and an edition with my story, 'Rhoda Kalema: Conquering Calamity through God's Grace', was published in Volume 5 Number 2 in June 2004.

In addition to all these, I have been conscious of the inevitable fact that I am ageing, every year, and that it is now approximately 30 years since I started recording my life's experiences.

In this book, I have attempted to cover, to the best of my knowledge, ability and memory, my childhood, education, marriage, parenthood and family. I have narrated the story of my life as a public servant, political and civil activist, my voluntary work as well as my spiritual journey.

Life is a wonderful gift. It is amazing how much of what is stored in one's memory comes to the surface when one is provoked to write their story. You too, reader, have a story that is waiting to be told.

Reverend Selywn Hughes, founder of the daily devotional publication, *Every Day with Jesus*, states that in all that happens to us, in our short or long lives, a bigger story is being written by God. As I write this, God is still writing my story even without me realising it.

Now, let me take you to where my story began.

Chapter 1

Early Years

I was born on 10th May 1929, at Mengo Hospital, in Kampala, to Martin Luther Nsibirwa and Veronica Namuddu. My father had several wives as polygamy was a normal tradition in those days, particularly among chiefs. So I grew up in a large family with many brothers and sisters. It is said that 'tradition dies hard' so although conversion to Christianity did not end polygamy immediately, other common cultural practices that existed then, such as drinking of alcohol and beliefs in witchcraft and superstition, were absent in our home. My father loved God and would go to church every morning. He insisted on holding daily evening family prayers which he led. He instilled the fear of God into his children.

Mengo Hospital is on Namirembe Hill, which is adjacent to Mengo Hill, the capital of the Buganda Kingdom where the Kabaka (King) had his main palace. Founded by Albert Ruskin Cook, a Church Missionary Society (CMS) missionary, in 1897, Mengo was the oldest hospital in Uganda, and, indeed a pioneer hospital in East Africa. By the time I was born, the hospital had the leading maternity facilities in the country, including a midwifery training school.

A month before I was born, my father became the Katikiro (Prime Minister) of the Kingdom of Buganda. Buganda is the

1

central kingdom from which Uganda, the country, derived its name. He was Katikiro from 1929 to 1941 and served again from 7th July 1945, to 5th September 1945.

My father, a member of the *Nvuma* clan – one of the fifty-two clans of Buganda – was from a large family. The clan system defines Kiganda society and every clan is represented by a totem. *Nvuma* is a seed of an underwater plant called *omuvuma*. In our culture, a person takes their father's clan and is given a name from among those reserved for their clan. Born in Kirindi, Bugerere, my father was the fourth-born of ten children – seven boys and three girls. As I was growing up, I remember his three sisters – Susana, Erina, and Mirika. Susana and Erina were married, but Mirika and one of his brothers, Makaya, never married and they lived with us in our big home.

Although she died when I was very young, I knew that my father loved his mother, Bulyaba, dearly. All I know about his father, Kiwana, is that he was one of those who volunteered to carry materials for the building of the first church on Namirembe Hill, which later became the Namirembe Cathedral. One day, as he was struggling with a heavy pole, it fell on him and he suffered serious injuries which he later succumbed to. Two of my siblings, Kiwana and Bulyaba, were named after my father's parents.

My father married his official wife, Damali, in church around 1904 when he was about twenty years old. Damali, who was known as *Mukubwa* (the senior one) accepted the other wives as they arrived and they accorded her due respect. This was the custom in Buganda then. Christianity, with its strictures against polygamy, was just being established. The other wives were Veronica Namuddu, Erina Nankya, Kasalina Ntabade, and Naome Kipanda. *Mukubwa* had a prime place though; she had her own quarters in the *Butikiro*, the official residence of the Katikiro.

The other four wives had their own quarters in the *Butikiro* homestead, where they lived with their children. Nonetheless, all the children worked, played and did everything together during the day. Wherever mealtimes found us, there we would sit and have the meal with 'our mother' – it did not matter which one.

Father administered a very well regimented homestead and our family included his wives and their young relatives, his children, nephews and nieces and male relatives whom he educated. Being the outstanding one in his family, he was generous and he happily took care of every person he regarded as his own.

Although he was devoted to his children, Father was a tough disciplinarian. He never tired of teaching us the importance of respecting others. Absolute honesty was central to his life and he constantly told us how important it was to have a sense of shame. "A person without a sense of shame is not a human being," he would tell us. Curiously, he did not believe in punishing his relatives' children. "How do I know how that behaviour came about?" he would ask. All the same, all relatives living with us had to learn the expected family 'behaviour' – and learn fast.

Father was very strict about our school performance. The first evening of each holiday was the time for reading school reports. Although he barely spoke or understood the English language, he strictly followed the teachers' comments. He disliked expressions like "Could do better" (*kuudu* for him) and "fair" (*foya*) as he pronounced these words. "It means not good enough!" He would point out. We had the discomfort of explaining why, indeed, we had not performed better in our studies.

Father took time to interact with us. He would set aside exclusive moments for his many children and he always communicated clearly and directly. There were also light moments when he would have fun teasing us.

I will always remember the school holiday, around 1942 while staying at our Kirindi home in Bugerere County when, out of the blue, my father 'ordered' me to accompany him to Namakomo, our country home in Kyagwe County (present-day Mukono District), which was under the care of his lovely widowed cousin, Yayeri. I was about thirteen years old, the age when impressions can leave a lifelong impact. I had him almost all to myself for three days! While we were there, he lost his uncle, Semioni Kalulwe. We got into the car and went to the funeral, about 15 miles away. Looking back, I see that, to my father, I was as valuable and as able as anyone else – son or daughter, young or old.

I was the fourteenth of twenty-seven children. They are, in birth order with married names in brackets, Maliyamu Nakimu (Kafeero), Tito Gita, Lusi Nvumirwa (Kibirige), Kasalina Mbekeka (Lule), Yayeri Nanozi (Mukibi), Paulo Munyagwa, Janet Nkabidwa (Mdoe), Sira Bugembe, Alistaluko Kiwana, Kosai Waggwa, Joyce Nakalema (Serunjogi), Eresi Namayanja (Lutalo) and Sara Nabwami, the thirteenth-born whom I followed. After me were Semu Ntulume, Eseza Kakoba (Kironde), Gladys Bulyaba (Wambuzi), Samwiri Kasirye, Isiraeri Senkirikimbe, Deborah Gwera (Sentongo), John Seruwagi, Philipo Lugolobi, Robinah Nankanja (Serwada), John Mugabi, Leah Nagita, John Sendagire and Rosemary Namusisi (Kigonya).

My mother, Veronica Namuddu, was from a small but close-knit family. As I was growing up, she often talked about a brother, Samwiri Mugwanya and an older sister, Magdalene, but I never met them; they died when I was young. She told us that after she got married and before I was born, her sister, Magdalene, would visit and assist her with chores around the home, especially digging in the garden. Mother dearly loved her brother's children – Katumba, Ida, Jeneti, and Edisa. She took care of them after the death of their mother so we grew up with them and we were very close.

Mother was a very important influence in my life. Her great love and care for me, for all my sisters and brothers and the members of her family, still resides in my memory. I remember how she spent a lot of time and energy ensuring that we were well fed and comfortable, especially when we were about to go back to school. I will always remember her monitoring our temperature by touching our foreheads or necks when my siblings and I were feverish. Her grandchildren were also extremely dear to her as she was to them. They enjoyed sharing funny jokes.

Mother loved her family and she also welcomed everyone who came her way. She was generous and kind and made friends easily. To her, being friendly was a duty and she saw the goodness in everyone. Her amicable personality contributed greatly to the harmonious atmosphere in our large family.

Many people from Busoga, a neighbouring region and Rwanda, had settled near our Bugerere country home, in Kayunga District where mother settled after father retired in 1941. Because she believed she had to communicate with everyone around her, she always endeavoured to speak other languages, including Lusoga, Kinyarwanda, Runyankore, and

Kiswahili. She even tried speaking English and she would boast that she knew 'Ingilisi'. Having attended an elementary vernacular school, the highest standard at the time, I remember how, well into her early eighties, she read the national Luganda papers daily, although she could only labouriously write her name.

Despite her pleasant, kind and approachable behaviour, mother was very strict about her children doing the right thing, being well-behaved, showing respect to, and caring for others. When it came to our education, she was extra serious. I recall a time when my brother, Kiwana, who wanted to join King's College Budo like his older brothers, refused to go to Mengo High School. He hid in the drainage pipes next to Butikiro House on Kabakanjagala Road. Mother looked for him and when she found him, she made him go to school. At the end of the year, he was sent to Budo.

Mother taught me the importance of living a practical life. She was organised and always busy from early morning till late evening. During the school holidays, I always wanted to be around her as she carried out her duties. I would follow her to the garden in the morning, and cultivate beside her. Later, we would harvest some food, take it home and prepare lunch. Mother always prepared extra food at lunchtime just in case we got unexpected visitors. In the evenings, we would return to the garden to attend to lighter work like weeding, picking vegetables and collecting banana leaves for cooking the next day's *matoke* (green bananas), the Buganda staple. Whenever the seasonal crop was ready for harvest, she would ask us to take maize, beans, or *lumonde* (sweet potatoes) from her garden to her neighbours. I learnt from her how to run a home and relate to the people around me.

After the death of our father, Mother settled in Kamuli, Bugerere County and became a councillor at the *gombolola* (sub-county) council at Kangulumira. She instilled in us the importance of hard work and service.

Mother loved the church and I have fond memories of our attending church together. In due course, she offered a piece of land to St James Church which is near her home in Kamuli.

My mother died on 12th March 1991 at the age of eighty-seven. Her whole life is a wonderful memory for all in our family.

The Buganda of My Father

Christianity, and the white man's world it introduced, was only eight years old in Buganda when my father was born around 1883. Mutesa I, the then reigning Kabaka of Buganda, was farsighted. In his April 1875 letter addressed to Queen Victoria of England, which he gave to Henry Morton Stanley, he requested that she send him personnel to enlighten his subjects and teach them about God. The letter which was written in Luganda read:

BUGANDA KINGDOM

The Lubiri - Lubaga 14-4-1875

To Queen Victoria in London

King of the Kingdoms of Europe which I hear about,

I have written giving you great respect and honour, and with my people, princes and princesses, all the chiefs and heads of clans of my country, greet you with great honour.

I, with all my people's chiefs, princes and princesses, write to you in trust that you may send us the understanding and wisdom from the books of your country as it is with your people.

I ask that you send me experts in wisdom and understanding to come and teach all my people all the wisdom you have in your country. Send me trustworthy people who will not betray my country or confuse my people into indecent behaviours BUT will help my people and myself in getting wisdom which will enable me to rule and bring my land to great peace.

You should also send me teachers of religion that I may understand God.

I

Mutesa (Mutesa I).

Then affixed his left hand thumbprint on the letter.

Kabaka Mutesa I died on 5th October 1884. At the time of his death, he was an international figure. *The Times* of London wrote about the passing away of a 'remarkable man.' Buganda and, later, the nation of Uganda, would consider his quest for enlightenment to be his main legacy.

The death of Mutesa I ushered in the reign of his son, Mwanga in October 1884. Kabaka Mwanga II was very different. He was only eighteen when he ascended the throne. Youthful, impetuous and not given to taking advice from elders, he was thrown, unprepared, into a world of changing power structures. Christian teachings and the Western world, Islamic converts and traders from the Muslim world were all pulling in different directions. Traditionalists were also clamouring for the Kabaka's ear. In trying to strengthen his position, Mwanga ended up alienating all the factions. He also started killing Christian converts known as 'readers' who would later come to be known as the Uganda martyrs.

Between 1888 and 1892, religious wars exploded in Buganda as the different factions fought each other. For ten years, the region was engaged in wars that may have been started on the pretext that they were religious, but as Samwiri Karugire explains:

> The wars in Buganda married religion to politics in
> a manner that was to prove irreversible in the whole
> of Uganda up to the present day. The factions who
> were battling it out in Buganda were not fighting
> for the protection of their faiths, but rather for the
> political control of Buganda.[1]

By the end of the century, the balance of power had changed. The king's power was weakened. Mwanga, who had been deposed, was restored to the throne before he was captured in Lango, Northern Uganda, alongside his old enemy, Kabalega, the Omukama (King), of Bunyoro. The Protestants and the British were in charge in Buganda, the defeated Catholics were quiet – on the sidelines – while the Muslims were in exile in Ankole, Bunyoro and Northern Uganda. The Bunyoro Kingdom, Buganda's old-time rival to the north-west, was defeated and broken and her southern counties of Buyaga and Bugangaizi torn away and given to Buganda. Mwanga and Kabalega were exiled to the Seychelles Islands in the Indian Ocean. Mwanga died in the Seychelles in May 1903 and Kabalega died on his way home in 1923. The British consolidated their hold, first on Buganda, then on the wider Uganda.

Within Buganda, there was a new Kabaka on the throne, Daudi Chwa II, who was born in August 1896. He was barely two years old when he succeeded his father. To assist

---

1   Samwiri R. Karugire, *The Roots of Instability in Uganda* (Kampala: Fountain Publishers, 1996), p. 13.

him were three regents; Apolo Kagwa the Katikiro (Prime Minister), Zakaria Kizito Kisingiri the Muwanika (Treasurer) and Stanislaus Mugwanya the Mulamuzi (Chief Justice). The real power resided with the Katikiro, Apolo Kagwa. The young Kabaka Chwa II never really came out of his regents' shadows – even in adulthood – as long as Apolo Kagwa was in charge.

In 1895, when my father was about twelve years old, he was christened Martin Luther and became a member of the Anglican Church. Buganda's religious wars were coming to an end around that time, and the Anglicans were in control in Buganda. My father's maternal uncle, Temutewo Mulondo, took him to be apprenticed as a page in the household of Katikiro Apolo Kagwa. This move determined the course of his life.

Pages attached to the households of chiefs acquired an informal education, administrative and political skills. They were also taught public speaking and how to endure hardships. Nsibirwa taught himself how to read and write by looking at the letters he delivered to chiefs as he ran errands. He also had the opportunity to work with land surveyors and learn their craft. Since his work entailed being sent all over Buganda, he got to know the whole kingdom well.

The establishment of the British Protectorate of Uganda in 1894 was the precursor to the 1900 Uganda Agreement that was also known as the Treaty of Mengo. The agreement not only defined the relationship between the Kingdom of Buganda and the Uganda Protectorate, it also brought into existence within the then British Empire, an entity known as Uganda.

Meanwhile, the spread of the Christian religion resulted in the profileration of a new order around the country. Wherever church leaders or lay preachers settled, they would establish churches and schools. Health centres would spring up around the churches. Chiefs, led by the Katikiro, brought new knowledge that transformed people's lives. They educated people on modern agricultural techniques and taught them how to grow food and cash crops, including cotton and coffee. The chiefs also organised the people and they worked on communal labour projects, known as *bulungibwansi* (for-the-good-of-the-nation), especially roads.

Sir Apolo Kagwa's long administration as Katikiro ended with his resignation in July 1926. When he died in February of the following year, the *East African Standard* of 1st March 1927, wrote:

> Thus has passed into the shadow one of the greatest African statesmen that has ever lived. If the Baganda as a nation will only follow his example, they need never fear for the future of their country... He stands out as a leader in civil and political life. After hours spent in meetings, he would be found writing the minutes of the discussions and yet, in spite of these labours, he would collect information about his own people and ancestors and not least, relax with his family and attend the religious services.

Apolo Kagwa was succeeded by Tefiro Kisosonkole whose term lasted two years. Meanwhile, my father who had risen steadily in Buganda's administration service from a *gombolola* (sub-county) chief for Kasawo in Kyagwe County, had by 1927, served four terms as *saza* (county) chief for both Bugerere and Singo. He had had an excellent mentor in Apolo Kagwa and he had also proved his bravery when he led the hunt for and eventually killed a lion that was terrorising villagers in Bugerere. "I cannot afford to be fearful when serving my King," he stated afterwards.

When my father was called upon to serve as the Muwanika (Treasurer) of Buganda under Katikiro Tefiro Kisosonkole, he said in his acceptance speech, "Even though I did not learn money matters, my King, I will take good custody of Buganda's money." He fulfilled his pledge and built up a rich treasury. My father must have been a good public servant because he was elevated to the position of Katikiro after only two years when Kisosonkole retired in April 1929.

In May of that year, I came into the world.

From historical accounts, my father was appointed to the office of Katikiro at a time when the country needed a person like him. He led a demanding public life, characterised by a series of tough decisions that would earn him lifelong admirers as well as enemies.

At the end of the 1920s, Buganda was at the end of one era and the beginning of another. It, therefore, needed a man who could ensure stability amidst change. Being a disciplinarian and an authoritative figure, my father had the steadiness that was required at the helm. A just man, he would listen attentively to his subordinates and even to those he considered his enemies. He was trusted with ensuring that change took place smoothly even when he was not completely conversant with the new world that was being ushered in.

Childhood memories of our home

I have many happy memories of my childhood in our large home. *Butikiro* House, the Katikiro's official residence, was built when I was about four years old. It was built after *Twekobe*, the main house in the Kabaka's *Lubiri* (palace enclosure). It was built outside the *Lubiri*, opposite *Twekobe*. My clearest memory of the *Butikiro* House construction is of two tall Sikh men with big white turbans on their heads. I also remember the big concrete mixer that made a lot of noise as it turned round and round. The huge house with walls that were several blocks thick and the deep, round underground tank that was used to store rainwater from the roof of the house form a significant part of my childhood memories.

Several faithful stewards who were our father's home staff also come to mind. There was Yakobo Nsubuga, the main steward who lived with his wife, Victoria, and family in a separate house within our large compound. He was in charge of finances and ran everything, including providing necessities for our mothers, all the children and relatives. Then there was Anderea, who was tall, pleasant and always clad in an impeccably clean white *kanzu* (long-sleeved ankle-length tunic of Arab origin). His sole duty was taking care of our father's laundry.

I particularly remember Leo Sebingi, a close relative, whose main job seemed to be one of ferrying sick children to the hospital on his bicycle. I suffered a malaria attack when I was about eight and the doctor at Mulago Hospital prescribed daily injections for about two months. Sebingi would cycle with me daily seated on his bicycle carrier to Mulago about four miles away. Unending daily trips, ferrying a sick child to hospital must have been draining; to me, it proved his faithfulness. I remember the very tender care he showed me. After the sickness, my mother told me that I built an immunity to malaria. Sebingi's daughter, Allen Nvumirwa, attended the same school with one of my sisters and, growing up, she was one of my best friends.

Then there was Malaki Matovu, my father's faithful driver who always drove us to boarding school and back at the beginning and end of every term. One of my earliest memories of him is his wedding to Mary, my mother's relative, when I was five years old. Malaki was with my father on the morning of 5th September 1945, when my father was assassinated. I am still in touch with Malaki's two sons.

Yokana Sendagire, a very close *Nvuma* clan relative of my father, was fairly educated and lived with his family in the Kisenyi area outside the *Butikiro*. Sendagire was my father's close adviser on money, land and clan issues so when my father was killed, Sendagire proved to be very useful when it came to sorting out inheritance and land issues – given the large size of our father's family. He was the closest uncle that we could relate to. His son, John Kasirye, was my brother Kiwana's classmate at King's College Budo.

Erisa Mukasa, also a *Nvuma* clan relative, was another close aide to our father. His home was in Nsangi in Busiro County, about twelve miles from Mengo. I cannot remember his specific duty in our home, but one significant event stands out – his daughter Aida Nantale's marriage to Mr Kibirige in 1935 during which my sisters, Eresi, Sara and I were her bridesmaids. Together with Yokana Sendagire, he was very helpful in sorting out our land inheritance issues; they both knew intimate details about our father's estate.

Chapter 2

Education and Growing Up

My elementary education started when I was about five years old, at a kindergarten within the *Lubiri*. The church in the palace grounds served as a kindergarten on weekdays for the children of the chiefs who lived around Mengo and near the palace. Among them were the Kisosonkole, Kitakule, Kitamirike, and Musajjalumbwa families. I went to the kindergarten with my sisters Sara, Eseza, and Gladys, and my brother Semu. We learned counting and the Luganda alphabet starting with the vowels A-E-I-O-U. My sister Janet recalled years later, that the school fees at that time, was one shilling (Sh. 1.00).

In 1936, my father decided to send my sister, Sara Nabwami, and I to Gayaza High School about twelve miles north east of Kampala, for Primary One. It was the leading and oldest girls' school around. Founded in 1905 by the CMS, it was set up to train young women to become excellent wives for leaders in society. After one year though, my father decided to send us to King's College Budo, the first co-educational school.

King's College Budo, was founded in 1906 by the Anglican CMS to cater mainly for the education of chiefs' sons. It was founded by the Reverend Henry W. Weatherhead and Bishop Alfred R. Tucker, the first Anglican Bishop of

Uganda. Weatherhead served as the school's first headmaster until 1911.

The two scouted around fourteen sites before settling on Budo, a flat and expansive sacred hill west of Kampala where Kabakas are crowned. Boldly, they approached Sir Apolo Kagwa and asked for the land. According to records, Reverend Weatherhead reported, "I blatantly told Apolo that I will take Budo or nothing."[2] He got the hill.

Co-education was a revolutionary concept. It had been introduced in 1933 with just twelve girls by the then headmaster, Canon Harold M. Grace. Sara and I, and our younger sisters, Eseza and Gladys, who joined in 1938, were afforded this amazing opportunity, one that would open doors that were, at that time, closed to most women around the world.

Being at Budo meant growing up and learning alongside boys and young men, a thing that was, hitherto, almost taboo. It would mean all the rough bits – competing, arguing and fighting – as we learnt to live together in mutual respect. It would stretch my capacity to match the standards set for all. At Budo, I was to be groomed to take on the world of men.

When my sister and I joined the school, with Alex Musoke and Mary Kulubya, we were about thirty girls. Sara and I were privileged to have older brothers in the school. It ensured that we were checked on constantly. The matrons were dutiful and motherly and we felt as if we were in a 'home away from home'. The headmaster, Canon Lewis J. Gaster, kept a close watch over all the girls. At times, when it rained, he would ferry us in his car from the girls' end to the main school.

---

2   Gordon P. MacGregor, *King's College, Budo: The First Sixty Years* (London: Oxford University Press, 1967), p. 9.

At Budo, one's social status was completely irrelevant; it did not matter who you were. For instance, Omulangira (Prince) Edward Mutesa, the future Kabaka of Buganda, was once rapped with a ruler on his fingers by teacher Samwiri Nkata in class. His middle finger was injured and it was treated. It is said that when his father, Kabaka Chwa II, learnt about the punishment, he firmly told his son, "Well, the teacher wanted to teach you not to play in class," and that was the end of it.

In 1939, when I was in Primary Four and ten years old, three significant incidents took place in quick succession. The first was the start of World War II, on 1st September 1939, when Germany invaded Poland. The War ended in 1945 when I was sixteen years old. The second incident was the death of my sister Sara. The third was the death of Kabaka Daudi Chwa II on 22nd November 1939 and his son, Mutesa, becoming the new Kabaka. While the first incident did not directly affect me, the other two left significant impressions on my life at that young age.

However, it is worth noting that when World War II broke out, Uganda, as a British Protectorate, got involved and the burden of wartime responsibilities was heavy on my father. These included recruiting of young men into the army. I remember two of my brothers, Paulo and Sira, as well as three relatives of my father's wives, going to fight in Burma.

Death of my sister Sara

My sister Sara died near the end of our third year at Budo. It was a tragedy, not just to our family, but to me in particular. Budo, set on a high, rocky hill overlooking Lake Victoria, is susceptible to lightning. In its history, lightning has struck the

17

school grounds a notable number of times, but without tragic consequences.

Normally, on Saturdays, we had free time in the course of which we washed our clothes, played and rested after lunch. On the afternoon of 10th October 1939, Sara, our friend Alice Tabu Zirabamuzale and I went to play outside the Gaster Dormitory. We built a small grass 'hut' and were asleep in it when we were suddenly woken up by a loud crash of thunder. Tabu and I followed other students, who were running in blind terror towards the dormitory. When we got in, our matron, Miss Juliana Namala, on checking to see whether anyone was missing, asked us frantically, "Where is Sara?" We answered, "Sara was sleeping; we left her."

"Sleeping?" she cried, as she ran outside. There, in the small makeshift grass hut, Sara lay still, like one who was asleep. Miss Namala shook her and called her name. She did not respond. Tabu and I did not know that when we left the hut, Sara had been struck and killed by lightning.

The death of Sara was a great shock to the whole school. I was overwhelmed with grief. I was broken. With only a year's age difference between us, we were very close. She would have turned eleven the next day. She and I had done everything together. She was not only my sister, but was also my closest friend.

From then on, I had to learn to live without her. It was difficult because there were things that I could not share with anyone else, not even with my other sisters. They would not have understood – there was a bigger age difference between them and us. Eventually though, in addition to Alice Tabu, I made other lifelong friends. We named our fifth child Sara, after my sister. Almost all of my siblings named a child after Sara.

Death of Kabaka Daudi Chwa II

Shortly after my sister's death, Kabaka Chwa II died at the age of forty-three. It was the heavy responsibility of the Katikiro to announce the death to the nation. I was only ten at the time, but I remember my father leading the preparations for both the dead Kabaka's funeral and the declaration of the new Kabaka.

Kabaka Daudi Chwa's death was, in a way, the end of an era. His reign had been peaceful compared to the turbulence that had characterised the rule of the previous Kabakas. He, however, had lived his whole life in the shadow of regents, led by the Katikiro. The young king, therefore, had not experienced any violent changes. Although a calm man, he passionately protected Baganda customs and culture from outside influences. He did not agree entirely with the colonial administration and his stand on many issues had an impact on their relationship.

On the economic front, Kabaka Chwa II presided over remarkable developments. The 1920s and 1930s were decades of accelerated transformation for Uganda. Newspapers and the radio spread news quickly around the country and roads, administrative centres, towns, schools, churches and hospitals were established countrywide. The East African Railway (originally the Uganda Railway), which had reached Kisumu from Mombasa in 1901, linked landlocked Uganda to the rest of the region and the outside world. In 1927, Kabaka Chwa II broke ground for the laying of the railway tracks that would connect Njeru (near Jinja) to Kampala. This reduced the travel time of the 716-mile journey from Kampala to Mombasa from two months to two days.

Prince Edward Frederick David Walugembe Mutesa, was only fifteen years old when he succeeded his father as Kabaka

Mutesa II. He ruled under regents just like his father until he was enthroned at the age of eighteen. My father and his successor Samwiri Wamala, were chief regent and, therefore, answerable to the Protectorate Government on all major issues.

Secondary School Life

In 1941, I was in Primary Six, which was then the highest grade in primary school. This was also the year that the public Primary Leaving Examinations were introduced countrywide. Our class of 1941 were the pioneers. Before that, pupils just moved on to secondary school. There were seven girls in Budo that year and, in the exam, I was the top student among the girls. I also won the needlework prize. The top boy was Spencer Kamulegeya. Spencer and I were awarded a Budo Junior Secondary School scholarship that would cover Junior I to III. Students from other schools also joined Budo at this stage after passing an entrance test. The class grew larger and we were thereafter split into A and B streams. I was with Mary Kulubya and Bitijuma Sekagya in stream A. Mary was one of my closest friends. She was a tall friendly girl who loved swimming. Bitijuma later became a primary school teacher and taught for a long time at the Police Training School in Nsambya.

I was thankful to John Bulwanyi (later, Dr John Bulwanyi), who was my class neighbour in J.III for the help he gave me in mathematics. I enjoyed all the subjects including arithmetic, but not the fearsome algebra and geometry, chemistry and physics. What I achieved in algebra and geometry in the J.III final exam, I owe to him.

In addition to academic subjects, boys learnt carpentry while girls studied domestic science and needlework in junior secondary classes. We studied the basic principles of cookery, housewifery and laundry – skills that have served me well.

At the end of 1944, I passed the Junior III examinations and qualified for Secondary four to six. I was fifteen at the time. Before the examinations, my older sister Janet Nkabidwa and Alistaluko Kiwana, my brother, expressed concern about my future and they offered to guide me. This was because they were aware that career choices, even for male students, were limited.

As far as career choice was concerned, I did not want an academic course that would lead to Makerere College because that meant that I would have to study the maths, physics, and chemistry subjects that I dreaded. Kiwana suggested that I go into nursing while Janet, who was a teacher, suggested I go for teacher training. Their options held no appeal for me and I also did not wish to go to Nsuube Domestic Science College, a popular institute for girls at the time. Finally, I decided to take a commercial course that was offered at Budo, and which today would be known as Business Studies. At that time, the course was favoured by boys, especially those who, like me, were not keen on the advanced maths and science subjects. The three-year course offered subjects like typing, shorthand, book-keeping, office routine, commercial geography, plain arithmetic, and commerce. Its graduates readily found employment in offices as clerks.

I was curious about the typewriter – the computer of the time. Commercial students learned to type on the keyboard while listening to Scottish country dance music, which made the course even more appealing for me. Kiwana encouraged me, but was cautious about my choice because I was setting a precedent – a girl enrolling in a commercial course. My hurdles were not yet over. The headmaster, Mr Dennis Herbert, did not want to risk admitting me into the commercial course class in case my father objected. Nevertheless with my brother's assurance to Mr Herbert, I was admitted into the Senior IV Commercial Course in January 1945. All the same, the admission letter contained a caution:

> 26 December 1944
>
> Dear Mr. Nsibirwa,
>
> I am very glad to tell you that Rhoda has passed the Junior Secondary leaving examination and will be promoted to Secondary 4 next term "if you agree to her taking the commercial course" (this addition was handwritten).
>
> Yours sincerely,
>
> D G R Herbert
>
> H.M.

Being a progressive man, my father did not have any problem with my admission. He was just happy that I was 'going to type letters like men' (all clerks were men at the time).

In class, I was the only girl among nine male students in the commercial stream. The other stream, known as the straight academic stream, had two girls, Lucy Mulyanti and Mary Kulubya. Later in life, I realised that due to my choice, I had the privilege of having many "brothers" – thirty-five altogether – from the academic and commercial classes of 1945 to 1947. I stayed in touch with most of them as they pursued their respective professions; two became medical doctors, one a dentist, one a veterinary doctor and the others joined the civil service in various capacities.

After three years of training, I received three academic certificates, for the eleven years at Budo – a Uganda Commercial Secondary Leaving Certificate; a London Chamber of Commerce Full Certificate; and a King's College

Budo Leaving Certificate. As was expected, the final day in school was emotional, as I was leaving the place that had nurtured me for eleven out of my eighteen years of life.

Other Budo Memories

Looking back, I have many fond memories of Budo where, in addition to the academic studies, we lived a free and full life. There were games and other social activities. I particularly enjoyed rounders and netball, community service in the neighbourhood, house debates, swimming, and Saturday evening concerts. Above all, I learnt to relate to boys and girls alike.

In school, we shared almost everything that youngsters were wont to do – we even shared our punishments. One Saturday evening, while walking back from a house concert at the upper end of the school, the mood among a group of girls was one of excitement. There was loud talk and laughter and some girls in the group, seeing that our matron, Miss Naome Naigwe was escorting girls in the dark, dared to throw stones at her. The stones were thrown in jest, and fortunately, they did not land on her. However, she was shaken and understandably, very angry. My friend Alice Tabu and a few other girls were identified as the culprits. On seeing Tabu, Miss Naigwe believed that I must have been part of the group. Try as we could, we failed to convince her otherwise. I shared the punishment without any bitterness.

Sunday morning services in the school chapel were very enjoyable. The combined boys' and girls' voices singing hymns and the daily morning quiet time in the dormitories laid the foundation for my spiritual life. The choruses taught by Ms Agnes Williams during the evening prayers in the dormitories were also spiritually inspiring. I recall many of them and they lend a lot of meaning to my life even now. The Sunday walks, with all the girls walking in a group and the boys in dormitory groups, were always enjoyable and mind-broadening as we stepped outside the school boundary under supervision. When mangoes were in season, we would pick and eat them with great delight during the walks, causing Ms Williams, who considered our actions bad manners, much anguish.

The Girl Guides and the Brownies groups for the senior and junior girls, respectively, and the Boy Scouts and Cubs for the boys, bring to mind special memories. The club activities focused on building good character and enhanced our life skills. They were part of the extra curricular school programmes.

In my final two years, I was a leader. First, I was appointed House Monitor in Grace House and in my sixth and final year, the girls' prefect. This strong foundation in leadership served me well years later, on the national stage.

I believe no student leaves school without rich sentiments and respect for their teachers. The teachers at Budo and their wives – the British and Ugandans, and Mr Lugalya, the carpentry teacher, who was Kenyan – acted as both teachers and parents to all students. Regarding respect for teachers, my brother Kiwana often told us how, long after he left Budo, he met his former teacher, Mr Samwiri Nkata, on Makerere Road. Kiwana, who was smoking a cigarette, stopped, dropped the cigarette, and stepped on it before wearing a big smile ready to greet his former teacher. It was only after Mr Nkata had walked away after the happy encounter, that Kiwana moved from the spot where he had stubbed out his cigarette. Years after leaving Budo, he still respected and valued Mr Nkata's opinion.

I have visited my cherished school on different occasions - as a parent, a grandparent, and an alumna. I have been greatly intrigued by the growth in the number of girls – from twelve in 1933 to 570 in 2020 – evidence of how the school has developed since its inception 115 years ago.

Significantly, apart from The Cottage, a small house that the first girls lived in, all the girls' dormitories were named after the first three headmasters. Sabaganzi House was named after the founder of the school, Reverend Henry Weatherhead, whose nickname was *Sabaganzi* (Kiganda for 'the much loved'). Grace House was named after Canon Harold Grace who introduced co-education in 1933, and Gaster House was named after Canon Lewis Gaster who succeeded Canon Grace in 1934.

Having joined in 1937, I remember the construction of the second half of Gaster House and the first part of Grace House, in 1938. The foundation stone was laid by Lady Irene Druscilla Namaganda, the wife of Kabaka Daudi Chwa II. Sabaganzi House was built in 1945 by Polish released prisoners of war who came to Uganda as refugees during World War II. Today, all these houses have extensions and are filled to capacity.

My other special memory was the naming of the school-leaving classes. It had become the trend, from a time that I cannot remember, for the final secondary school class to have a special name. Perhaps this was to depict its 'importance' or 'strength'. Those immediately before us were the 'Stalwarts' and our 1947 class took on the name, the 'Vanguards'.

Remembering Miss Williams

It is befitting to conclude this chapter with a special mention of Miss Agnes Williams. She is one person I can never forget because she instilled in me the importance of honesty and also planted in me the seed of spiritual faith during my early years – as I have mentioned before – through her choruses. She was a tall, well-built Englishwoman. In 1940, she came from Japan and joined the staff at King's College Budo. A dedicated Christian, she was a member of the CMS and she regularly led the prayers in the school's chapel. Her main subject was mathematics, which she taught in the secondary section.

When she joined the school, the number of girls was still low and she was the first fully-fledged girls' warden. Before her time, matrons were in charge of the three girls' dormitories. The dormitories comprised The Cottage, which housed seniors, Grace House which was for secondary students and Gaster House that housed juniors. The position of the girls' warden henceforth became an important one. Miss Williams was charged with caring for, disciplining and teaching the girls 'good manners'. She ensured that we did not dodge chapel, games or Sunday walks and she also saw to it that the girls were neatly dressed at all times. She took us swimming, once a week, at a pool that was located down the hill.

We were amazed at how swiftly she carried her large size around as she policed us. Her favourite five words, when she was not happy were, "I am ashamed of you…" followed by a girl's name. Those words would make one feel ashamed and remorseful. Her smiles were very rare, but no girl doubted her genuine love and concern for every one of them.

Above all, she was wholly involved in the girls' evening prayers and when we sang, 'Keep me Shining Lord', 'Wide, Wide as the Ocean' and 'Oh Make Me Understand It', the words were accompanied by actions. Miss Williams impacted the life of the other girls as well and through the years, we often spoke fondly about her and sang the choruses that she taught us. I also taught my children some of the choruses and they loved them.

Miss Williams went to England soon after the end of the Second World War.

Chapter 3

Assassination of My Father

When I started the commercial course in 1945, two memorable events occurred. First, the second World War ended with the Germans' surrender on 7th May, 1945. Second, four years into his retirement, my father was recalled to the office of the Katikiro by the Kabaka, Sir Edward Mutesa II, on 7 July 1945. Two months later, my father was dead, felled by an assassin's bullet.

By the mid-1930s, some young Baganda men, who had been exposed to British education, became politically aware of and active in national affairs. Because the idea of a united Uganda was still vague, nationalist patriotism was termed "fighting for Buganda." Increasingly discontented and critical of the Colonial and the Buganda governments, these young activists readily aired their grievances; hence, by 1945, there was growing political unrest. It would be a decade though, before politicians from around the country built nationally embracing platforms.

From the start of the British colonial intervention in Uganda in the mid-1870s, Buganda took centre stage in politics. This was because, for national decisions made by the colonial government to succeed, they had to be supported by Buganda chiefs, ministers and, in particular, the Katikiro who wielded a lot of power over all resolutions. That is why the Katikiro is known, even today, as *Kamala Byona* (the ultimate decision maker). In the rapidly changing Uganda, the Katikiro became the one who absorbed the fallout and damage that resulted from conflicts. He stood where giant interests clashed.

Two very sensitive issues came to a head during this period. One was the announcement that the Kabaka's widowed mother wanted to remarry, and the other was the planned expansion and elevation of Makerere College to university status.

In 1941, the young Kabaka's mother, the Namasole (Queen Mother), Lady Irene Druscilla Namaganda, stated that she wished to remarry. This was against the traditions of the Buganda royal family and Kabaka Mutesa II wrote:

> My mother was a woman of character and not a traditionalist. She decided to remarry and gained the support of the Katikiro. There was great opposition. In such cases the Kabaka alone has the power to allow tradition to be broken – that is to say, to alter tradition. She was determined, so I gave her my support, and the remarriage took place. Even then, the Katikiro Martin Luther Nsibirwa was forced to resign by some of the chiefs.[3]

My father, together with Hamu Mukasa, a seasoned chief in Buganda who was the *Sekiboobo,* the *saza* (county) chief of Kyagwe, supported this change in tradition. The Protectorate Government also supported it. However, this decision aroused violent feelings and was never accepted by the *Lukiiko* (parliament) and most of the other chiefs. My father and Ham

---

3   Mutesa II (King of Buganda), *Desecration of My Kingdom* (London, Constable, 1967), p. 85.

Mukasa became deeply unpopular in the whole of Buganda. Finally, the increasing agitation turned the tide in the *Lukiiko*, and my father was forced to resign in July 1941. Lady Irene was stripped of her Namasole title and it was inherited by her sister Perepetwa Nabawesi.

After twenty-two years in public office as *gombolola* and *saza* chief and Muwanika in the Buganda Government before becoming Katikiro for twelve difficult years, my father left office peacefully. He settled at his ancestral birthplace and built a new home at Kirindi, in Bugerere County, where he spent his time doing what he enjoyed – growing cotton, soya beans and other cash crops. He planted a vast *lusuku* (plantation) of *matooke*, the standard measure of a stable, prosperous home. With his wives and children around him, he was happy in retirement. I remember that he expected us, his children, to work in the gardens and to harvest the crops during our school holidays and I especially remember harvesting cotton during the December holidays. I retain happy and precious memories of the time of white fields of cotton.

In October 1944, the original 1900 Uganda Agreement was revised with the aim of redefining the relationship between Buganda and the Protectorate Government. However, the British Resident (the British Administrator) had a difficult time trying to persuade the Baganda to revise one line under clause 15 of the 1900 Agreement, so that it would cover two proposed projects. One was the acquisition of land to expand Makerere College into the University of East Africa, and the other was the acquisition of land at Namulonge for agricultural research and particularly, of cotton-growing as an economic development project for the country. The Namulonge Agricultural and Animal Production Research Institute, later established in 1949, presented no problem because an enlightened landowner, Kitamirike Musajjalumbwa, donated the land that was required.

The expansion of the Makerere land was problematic. The Protectorate Government sought to acquire privately-owned land on and adjacent to Makerere hill. Among the landowners were several influential chiefs. The government offered to exchange the acquired land with other parcels of land that were within reasonable proximity. The landowners rejected the introduction of a new clause in the 1900 Agreement that would give the government the power to obtain land for public works or other purposes. The clause in the agreement stated that if less than ten per cent of land was acquired, it could be taken without compensation to the owner. Despite compensation being offered in the case of Makerere, most of the Baganda chiefs would hear none of it and they refused to negotiate away their individual pieces of land.

My father did not have any land around Makerere but he had land close to Mulago Hospital which he surrendered to allow for the construction of a nurses' hostel during the hospital's expansion. In exchange, he got land in the Kampala suburb of Kansanga. Given his strong belief in education, he considered it his responsibility to allow the government to achieve its objective and he, therefore, supported the proposed acquisition. The landowners objected vehemently and the hostile relationship between them and my father became even more aggravated.

Back in the Protectorate Government, Governor John Hall's development plans for Makerere College ground to a halt. Stuck, he realised that for the law to empower the Kabaka to acquire land, "for purposes beneficial to the nation", the Buganda government power structures would have to be changed, and that in itself was going to be a dangerous undertaking. The solution, he believed, lay in the removal of all the chiefs who opposed the proposal.

This is the situation that confronted young Kabaka Mutesa II in his third year on the throne. Faced by instability, Mutesa II sought the firm hand of his father's confidant. He, therefore, decided to woo and recall my father back to the position of Katikiro but my father was strongly against the idea. He must have known the heights to which popular anger against him had been whipped. Mutesa II wrote;

> Nsibirwa, who had been Katikiro before, was thought by the Governor to be the man with experience to run the country. He was reluctant to return and he came to see me personally and, as he had promised my father to help me at all times, accepted when I asked him. He was still unpopular from his part in the remarriage of my mother.[4]

The momentum that sought to make sweeping changes in Buganda's administration intensified. In mid-1945, the storm hit and Katikiro Samwiri Wamala, my father's successor, was removed from the office because of his alleged involvement in the riots that had errupted that year in January. Subsequently my father was recalled, re-appointed and sworn in as Katikiro on 7th July 1945. He went back ready for battle.

---

4   Mutesa II (King of Buganda), *Desecration of My Kingdom* (London, Constable, 1967), p. 90.

The first thing my father did upon his return was to remove, at 24 hours' notice, all the chiefs who had been involved in his removal in 1941. Immediately thereafter, the Protectorate Government formally asked for more land to expand Makerere College, setting the scene for the final showdown.

By then, the number of my father's enemies had grown and their fury had risen to boiling point. Such was the tension that he must have feared for his life. The *Lukiiko* passed the Land Revised Bill on 4th September 1945.

My father's Assassination

As always, my father set out to start his day with early morning prayers in church. That morning, he did not enter church immediately as was his habit. He stopped on the steps in front of the doors at the Namirembe Cathedral. It was later reported that he had arranged, the previous evening, to meet Mr Bunjo, a long-term confidante. As he stood there, a gunman, hidden in the shrubs in front of the entrance, fired a number of shots into my father's chest. He died instantly, falling on his face near the Cathedral steps. He had only been back in office for two months.

As investigations later revealed, the plot to kill my father on 5th September 1945 was well planned. The objective was to stop the passing of the bill that would make it possible for the government to aquire land by ensuring that he did not append his signature to it. Unknown to the plotters, he signed the bill as soon as it was enacted and it had already been passed into law.

The gunman, a man called Senkatuka, was apprehended as he ran downhill from the Cathedral and taken back to the scene of the crime. He was later charged with the murder, convicted and hanged. Looking back, my father's assassination was part of the nation's crisis.

This unprecedented incident shattered the whole country. The news spread like wildfire and my father's friends grieved with our family. The courtyard at our Nakulabye home was filled with people from near and far as the family fell into inconsolable grieving. "If only he had not taken up the Kabaka's invitation, we would still have him," they wailed. My brother, Semu, was walking from home unaware that our father was dead. When he heard the news, he removed his shoes and walked barefoot as did other male relatives as was required by Buganda culture when one was mourning a person who was close to him, such as a parent.

Father was buried near the spot where he had fallen, in the main cemetry on the Cathedral grounds. Bishop Stuart led the funeral service.

Incidentally, this calamity occurred shortly after a happy family occasion – the wedding of my elder sister, Eresi Namayanja, on the 30th of June, to Dr Yafesi Lutalo.

As the years passed, we were consoled by the fact that our father had died fighting for a cause: the building of a better country. Throughout his life, he stood up for what he believed in.

The land for which he died was obtained. In 1949, Makerere College acquired university status and changed name to Makerere College, University of East Africa. It was affiliated to the University of London. More than sixty years later, Makerere University remains the highest institution of higher learning in Uganda. A number of my father's children, grandchildren and great-grandchildren have honoured our family by graduating from Makerere University. In 1997, fifty-two years after his death, the University Council honoured my father by naming one hall of residence, "Nsibirwa".

Before his death, my father received two awards. In 1941, he received, from the British Government, the Member of the Most Excellent Order of the British Empire (MBE) awarded, in his case, for services rendered during World War II. He was also the recipient of the Order of the Shield and Spears, the highest honour in Buganda. It was presented by Kabaka Daudi Chwa II.

Surviving Father's Death

When our father died, I was only sixteen years old. His death left a gap and there was no supportive relative to fill it.

We, his children, suddenly faced the possibility of being ejected out of school for lack of school fees. However, none of us ever missed a day of school. My elder brothers, Sira Bugembe and Alistaluko Kiwana, somehow mobilised the finances required by selling some of their newly inherited land. It was a show of great sacrifice and family love. Our mothers held together and provided us with the love, moral and social support that we needed. Up to this day, I am thankful and amazed at how so graciously God provided for us. Sira, Kiwana, my elder sister, Janet Nkabidwa and later, my younger brother, Semu Ntulume, became the anchors in our family. Where our mothers felt helpless, they supported us all and they were very committed in managing our family's affairs.

When our father died, Janet was away and we all missed her. She had gone to Southern Sudan in 1944 to work as a missionary teacher. She taught at Yei Girls' School with Deborah Nakku until 1946. They were the first female Ugandan missionaries there.

When I received the news of my father's death, I was at the home of Kopuliano and Katolini Kibuka, in Mukono, where I had been invited to spend the school holidays. Kopuliano was a teacher at Bishop Senior School in Mukono and Katolini Kibuka (whom we fondly called Katie), was my sister Janet's good friend and former schoolmate. They had trained together at the Buloba Teacher Training College in the 1940s before they later taught at Gayaza High School. We later became relatives when Katie's brother, Erisa Kironde, married our sister, Eseza.

On the day my father was shot, my cousin, Kiwanuka, arrived at the Kibuka home bearing the news of my father's murder. He was very agitated and frightened. I remember that moment vividly. I was holding the couple's nine-month-old baby, Joy. Katie and Kupuliano comforted and supported me during that difficult time that followed and I could not have been at a better place. The Kibuka's was a deep Christian home. Kapuliano, the son of Reverend K. Kagwa was a staunch Christian while Katie had a personal faith that made her a very special person. She had the gift of compassion and at school her nick-name was '*Meemenungi*' (Goodheart). Besides the immediate solace that the couple provided, they continued to play an important role in my life for over forty years. Katie died on 12th March 1985 and Kapuliano on 21st April 1998.

Chapter 4

First Job, Conversion and Marriage

When I completed my commercial course in 1947, I was eighteen – the age of majority. Until then, I had lived a protected life, between a boarding school and a close-knit family home. Coming out, I was ushered into the adult world. Without a father to shield me, I felt that I was not ready to take on the rough life of Kampala's daily office routine. This anxiety was eased, though, by the fact that King's College Budo taught me how to live in a 'man's world', with all its challenges.

Looking back, Budo girls, even in those early days, had the self-confidence to do whatever they wished to do with a well-developed sense of judgement and independence and even jobs that were considered to be the preserve of men did not daunt them. My Budo background served me well when I needed to set up and run an office at Gayaza High School.

Secretary-Bursar Job at Gayaza

I had enrolled for Primary One class, twelve years earlier, at Gayaza High School. My links went deeper; it was also my elder sisters' former school. So when a job opening came up, the school was happy to employ me as a Secretary-Bursar. The boarding school environment offered the best setting for my untried skills and I felt at home as the older missionary teachers took me under their wings. Miss Nancy Harris Corby, the headmistress, took me on as her special project. She had taught my elder sisters so when I joined her staff, it felt like I already knew her. A devout Christian, Corby was an able administrator, a role that she executed with a lot of consideration towards the staff and students.

The office of the bursar was next to the headmistress' and I was in and out of her office many times on any given day. As a bursar and secretary, my typing, office routine and bookkeeping skills came in handy but I gradually lost my shorthand skills. The school had never had a trained person carry out those duties before. I used my training to establish an efficient system in the bursar's office and I made record-keeping, receipt writing and filing correspondence common office practices. I grew in confidence and experience daily in handling people and figures. I learnt how to work under great pressure, especially at the beginning of each term when parents were paying school fees. However, this ideal status was short-lived because I only spent two years at the school before William Kalema turned up and changed everything.

Warming up to William Kalema

If William Wilberforce Kalema had not been close to my two brothers after he joined King's College Budo, it is possible that he would not have led me to the altar.

In 1942, he joined Budo and became a resident in England House. As it turned out, my brother Sira was also in England House while another brother, Kiwana, was in the same class as William. He became good friends with the two so we were bound to meet, sooner or later.

When we finally met though, ours was not the proverbial love at first sight. I was thirteen years old and not overly excited about boys. In fact, I never really took much notice of his charm when I met him with my brothers. Being three years older and three classes above me, he was not attractive to my young mind. I thought he was far too old. Moreover, there were two boys in a lower class who were fighting for my attention and they seemed more appealing as boyfriends. Not one to be put down easily, he pressed on. My brothers had 'casually' encouraged him to go ahead with plans to approach me and so he 'casually' set himself on the idea of approaching me directly.

One day, he wrote a short letter to me using expressions I cannot recall. He then devised a way of getting it to me. He came up with a scheme that involved his housemate Musalenyooka, whose sister, Edisa Sendikwanawa, was my classmate. So one Saturday afternoon, Edisa got me to go for a walk away from the girls' end to the lower field where William also happened to be out taking a casual walk towards us. When we met, he stopped and engaged us in small talk. As we chatted, I was taken aback when he handed me a letter. Edisa did not look surprised though. Immediately thereafter, he turned and walked back to the boys' end.

The letter declared his feelings towards me. Perhaps the reason I cannot recall the expressions he used was because it was the standard adolescent love letter. However, I remember that he signed off, "With much love, Yours William Kalema." Needless to say, it did not yield the desired result. However, it made me more aware of him and as I got to know him better, I realised that William was gifted in many ways. Among his admirable attributes was that he could understand difficult

39

concepts with little effort, and he was able to explain ideas to others with relative ease. I also noted that he was not keen on sports and, with time, I would discover that he was a man with unmatched determination.

William Wilberforce Kalema was born on 11ᵗʰ June 1926, to Samson Magala and Erusa Nalubowa in Mulagi village, about eighty miles mid-west of Kampala, in Singo County, in what is now Kiboga District. He was of medium height, slender, dark and handsome. He belonged to the *Mpologoma* (lion) clan and was the fourth child and second son in a family of eleven children.

William started his education at Bamusuta Primary School, a village elementary school in Kiboga. It is there that he completed Class Four, the highest grade in most rural schools at that time. He walked the four miles from home to school and back, barefoot, daily. Years later, he said he remembered losing toenails en-route and, pointing at a rock in the middle of the road, he would tell me, "That rock is the reason my big toenails are missing." On completing Class Four, he told his father that he wished to continue with his education and so he got on a bus and set off for Mukono Primary School, in Mukono, a hundred miles away from his home, where he knew no one. He asked for directions to the school and on arrival, he walked straight into the headmaster's office and asked for admission. The headmaster, Mr Zirimenya, listened to his story and with an affectionate slap on William's cheek, he told him, "Young man, come tomorrow and study." And thus begun the next stage of his education.

At Mukono Primary School, William did his Class Five and Six, followed by the Junior Secondary Classes JI, JII, and JIII. While in Mukono, he lived with a schoolmate, Senkubuge, near the school, at the home of an elderly lady called Buzibwa. Senkubuge and William later became teachers and lifelong friends. They were forever grateful to the elderly Buzibwa who had housed them and for years, they visited her with gifts.

After Mukono, William set his sights higher. He wished to join King's College Budo but he did not have the fee that was required for the Budo entrance exam. He, therefore, approached a teacher at Mukono Secondary School, Enoka Mulira, who gave him the one shilling he needed. William travelled to Budo, sat the exam and passed. He joined Budo in January 1942. He never forgot Enoka Mulira's precious help.

In 1945, William joined Makerere College where he enrolled for a Diploma in Education. He successfully completed the three-year course in 1947. He then joined the teaching staff at Budo in 1948.

He never gave up on me and, fortunately for him, he was still friends with my two brothers. They encouraged him to try again and that is how, at the beginning of my second year at Gayaza in 1949, William visited me. He arrived with his good friend, William Rwetsiba, a fellow teacher at Budo. This time he had the air of a man who had made up his mind and who did not want to waste any time. From then on, he visited frequently and he even looked me up at our family home in Nakulabye. At that point, he did not look so old anymore. He also had no competition. I started growing fond of him, though taking my time.

One afternoon in 1949, during the April to May school holidays, as we sat chatting under a tree on Makerere's main sports field, William stated, "I wish to get married next year." This he followed with the question, "When are you getting married?" Although I had become fond of him, I was not ready for his question because we had just reconnected a few months earlier. However, when he frankly declared his intentions, I realised that I was already in love with him.

When I went back to school, I confided in Miss Corby and she was very happy for me and gave me her blessing. She encouraged and supported me as we moved towards the end of the school year. The wedding date was set for the beginning of 1950 and I left Gayaza at the end of 1949, armed with the prospect of a change in my marital status, and a spiritual transformation.

My Conversion and the Start of a Spiritual Journey

My conversion to a 'saved' Christian took place in 1949, when I was working at Gayaza. Although while growing up I was privileged to have a Christian background at home and at school, I did not know that every Christian believer still needed to know Jesus Christ as a personal Saviour and Lord. At school, I learnt about God's power of creation, His holiness and love. In church, I constantly heard about His plan for saving His lost children from sin. I believe this background provided a rich resource for my life's spiritual journey.

The new development in my Christian life was as a result of a spiritual revival that had emerged in 1935 in the form of a movement. Known as the 'East African Revival Movement,' it started in Gahini in Rwanda and swept throughout the entire East African region. It spread in two streams, one from eastern Rwanda and the other from western Uganda. The pioneers of the Revival in the region were Simeoni and Eva Nsibambi, William and Sala Nagenda, Lawrence and Julia Barnham, Yosiya and Dorokasi Kinuka, Erica and Geraldine Sabiti, and Joe and Decie Church. Joe was a medical missionary who had been sent to Gahini to build a hospital. They were known as

Abalokole (the born-again). The revival had a lasting impact on Protestant leaders in East Africa and beyond.

Of the *Abalokole* couples, William and Sala Nagenda were known to me since Sala's younger sisters, Jane and Toni Bakaluba, my schoolmates, used to talk a lot about their elder sister. Jane became one of my best friends. Later, William and Sala's son, Jim, and my eldest son, William, became good friends too.

In Uganda, the revival breathed a new spiritual life into the Anglican Church although, at first, it met a lot of resistance from a majority of the church leaders and the mainstream Church Missionary Society. This was because traditional Anglican Church culture did not believe in showing open enthusiasm and joy or open repentance for personal misdeeds. Also, cautious about the possibility of uncontrolled spread of the 'wrong teaching', the free sharing of the Word of God by anyone who just felt like it was discouraged. Since the Revival Movement promoted free sharing, this set the stage for a major clash.

Undoubtedly, the revival brought great zeal, joy and personal liberation in believers' lives. People were challenged into making personal commitments to Christ. Those who were converted repented their sins publicly and many paid back what they had stolen and called themselves 'The Saved' *or Abalokole*. The Revival's impact compares very well, I believe, with the Welsh Revival of 1904, that was led by Evan Roberts. By 1949, the revival had impacted many people in south-west and central Uganda.

One afternoon in July 1949, I went to *Twekobe* (the palace) in Mengo to visit Nabagereka (Queen) Damali Kisosonkole, the wife of Kabaka Edward Mutesa II. The Nabagereka and I were close friends during our school days at Budo and since we were also neighbours in Mengo on Kabakanjagala Road, we often visited each other during school holidays. Our friendship lasted until she died in July 2010.

At the palace, I met Princess Ruth Komuntale, the Princess Royal of the Tooro Kingdom who was also visiting (her title, *Batebe*, is the equivalent of *Lubuga*, the title given to the prime sister of the Kabaka, in Buganda). A convert of the Revival Movement, the princess loved the Lord with a burning passion and she immediately started talking to me about salvation. Although I cannot remember her exact words when she greeted me, I do remember that she challenged me when she stated, "Rhoda, you must get saved and go to heaven."

Sometimes, it is difficult to find words to explain some things. All I know is that from that moment on, I felt uneasy. God's mysterious ways will always be a puzzle to me and I know of many who have unexpectedly found themselves in His custody in a similar way. Who ever imagined that on a visit to a queen in her palace, God would send His messenger, a princess, to talk to me about my salvation? This is perhaps a bit similar to the Bible story of the apostle Philip who was told to go and meet an Ethiopian official on a desert road and explain the scriptures to him (Acts 8:26-40). It seems like there is an angel that guides a person's movements and directions when God plans to reveal Himself. Later, I would marvel at how conversion happens in the most unexpected of places, ways and people! It is difficult to anticipate the Holy Spirit's course.

On my way home, I opened my heart and I let the Lord in. I felt a new life within me. I felt free and possessed of a new joy. I was 'saved'. When I arrived, I promptly 'witnessed' to my fellow members of staff with whom I shared a house. One of the teachers, my friend and relative, Gladys Nansubuga, also accepted Christ the following day. From that time, my Christian life took on a new meaning. I learnt to acknowledge and to recognise the need to confess and repent my sins. I believed that Jesus died on the cross and that He shed His blood for me so I could gain eternal life!

Visit to International Evangelist William Nagenda's Home

During the August to September school holidays of 1949, Gladys and I were invited to the Nagenda's home at Namutamba, about fifty miles northwest of Kampala. I already knew that the home was the seat of the *Balokole*. I must admit that, at first, I was worried about being closely associated with them, as they were believed to be a 'fanatical' group. Although wary of a close relationship, I decided to honour the invitation.

It was my first visit to Namutamba and I was fascinated by the much-talked-about tea estates of Lee Wilson, as we drove through the area. On arrival, we were welcomed with great joy and love and the joyous singing of the *Balokole* anthem, *'Tukutendereza Yesu'* (We Praise You Jesus) which greeted every guest as they arrived. As we sang, William Nagenda remarked as he greeted us, "You had abandoned the singing of *Tukutendereza* to us for too long," to everyone's great amusement.

The Nagenda home was not very big and I wondered where they accommodated all the guests who were constantly in and out of the house. The dining table was at all times packed with food and people eating around it. Apart from the guests, relatives and friends, they also had six children. To me, this welcome displayed an open generosity that could surely only be explained by Christ's love.

Most of Namutamba's *Balokole* families held fellowship meetings late in the afternoon daily at the local church. The fellowships were dominated by repentance and 'walking in the light' which meant openly confessing personal temptations and weaknesses like envy, hatred, bad feelings towards others and other sins that could hinder Christians from thriving and freely enjoying the faith they confessed. I shall never forget that experience.

At times I felt shaky when I had to share my new-found spiritual life with people close to me, like my large family. Even more intimidating, I had to share my gift of salvation with William, my fiancé. We had just decided to get married three months earlier and I asked myself, "Will he understand my new situation? Will this not change our plans?" Many such questions went through my mind, and many 'brethren of the saved movement' clearly discouraged me from going ahead with the planned marriage. Some of them, however, said that perhaps God would make me a witness in my new home and they quoted 1 Corinthians 7:13-14, which talks about how a believing wife should not divorce the man because he would be 'sanctified' (made clean) by her.

I remember experiencing a certain degree of doubt. I wondered what the right course was. When I shared my good news of salvation with Nancy Corby, my boss, she said to me, "It is wonderful that you are newly experiencing God's love and at the same time, the love of a fiancé."

I also shared my concern with William Nagenda. Although he was an international evangelist and a leader in the Namutamba community, William was approachable, friendly and humble. He talked to me, in a personal way, about my new salvation and my planned marriage to a man who had not yet found personal salvation in Christ. He promised to pray for me, for God to guide me. His counsel was instrumental in helping me make up my mind about going ahead with the wedding.

Wedding and Return to Budo

As part of the pre-wedding activities, we had a simple and modest traditional *kwanjula* (introduction) ceremony. Fortunately, William did not require much introduction; he was already a good friend who visited frequently, so he was well known to my family. They had already accepted him and they welcomed him warmly. Many years later, this cultural ceremony has developed into an affair that is accompanied by elaborate, costly fanfare. The pre-wedding ceremony, the *kasiki,* was also not a big affair.

I vividly remember receiving a lot of support from my extended family on my very special day. My sister Janet provided tremendous moral and financial support with her little teacher's salary. She bought fabric and because she did not have a sewing machine, she hand sewed my four bridesmaids' dresses. The dresses could have been made by Ben Edebe, a renowned tailor in Katwe, who made my bridal dress, but my sister committed herself to the task. The pink dresses were worn by my three younger sisters, Eseza, Gladys and Rosemary and the daughter of a friend, Yacob Kasumba, who was the Mayor of Mengo Municipality. They made a beautiful bridal party. My cousin, Charles S. Mukasa, who was known as CMS, bought me the bridal crown that held the veil.

The wedding on 11ᵗʰ February 1950 at Namirembe Cathedral was conducted by Bishop Cyril Simon Stuart, who was the Bishop of Uganda from 1932 to 1952. He had confirmed William in the early 1940s at his home church, St Thomas Church, Bamusuta, in Kiboga. On his return to England, he was appointed Assistant Bishop of Worcester. Miss Nancy Corby accepted to be my matron of honour, despite her limited knowledge of our Baganda wedding traditions. My paternal aunt, Erina Nalunga Buliggwanga, was my official bridal aunt (*Senga*). She happily played the role, standing close by my side in church and at the celebrations that followed. Nelson Nkalubo Sebugwawo, William's great friend, was the best man. My brother, Sira, who had been dormitory mates with William, gave me away in church.

Namirembe Cathedral was filled by our families and friends and the loud organ and Cathedral choir made the ceremony a glorious occasion. Although I do not recall the sermon, I remember my choice, Psalm 128, was beautifully sang by the choir.

Our wedding reception was held in the Makerere College dining hall – the only one dining hall in the whole College at the time. Unlike the weddings of later years, the food consisted of tea, bread and small cakes. The wedding cake was made and gifted by Mrs Lorna Hillier, my domestic science teacher at Budo and the wife of Mr Hillier, the head of the commercial course and my former bookkeeping and typing teacher. The cake was a simple, big, one tier affair.

After the ceremony, I changed into a beautiful, short, pink flowered dress; it was my best dress for a long time. From the reception, we travelled to Nelson Sebugwawo's official home. He was the *gombolola* chief at Kayunga. We found another very joyful, well-organised reception there. The drumming and traditional dancing went on into the early hours of the morning. We spent the first week of our married life at the

Sebugwawo home.

Altogether, we enjoyed a lot of love and support at our wedding and I look back at the entire ceremony with much thankfulness to God.

***

Let me digress.

My life journey with Nelson and Catherine Sebugwawo began when I married their great friend, William Kalema.

The friendship between my husband and Nelson had started about ten years earlier when Nelson had been a sub-county chief in Kiboga, William a teenage school boy and his elder brother, Katerega, the sub-county clerk.

Catherine was a devoted wife and mother who embraced everyone, including friends who were brought home by her husband. They both loved William and when we got married, they loved me too and we became members of their large family. We shared all our joyful and sad family occasions with them. The result was that all our children grew up as one family. They were godparents to two of our children, and we too were godparents to their children. I lived in a family (mine) within a family (theirs), which was quite large. My world became all the richer and larger for it.

The love, trust and friendship continued into the second generation of our two families and when the Sebugwawo family established the Nelson Nkalubo Sebugwawo Foundation, my eldest son, William Samson Kalema, was appointed its Chairman.

Maama Catherine died on 12th January 2007 aged 88, while Mzee Nelson Sebugwawo, who was born in April 1912, died on 9th August 2015, aged 103. I am very thankful to God for the presence of this family in my life.

Chapter 5

Our Young Family

Getting married to a Budo teacher meant returning to King's College Budo, the very school where we met and which I had only left two years earlier, for Gayaza High School. It is where we made our first home. When I left Gayaza, Nancy Corby gave me a card with the following words from the Bible (Num 6:22-26, NKJV):

> *The LORD bless you and keep you:*
> *The LORD make His face shine upon you, and be*
> *gracious to you:*
> *The LORD lift up His countenance upon you,*
> *and give you peace.*

This priestly blessing, which God gave to Moses to tell to Aaron and his sons, was to be used to bless the children of Israel. I kept the card for a long time and the beautiful prayer has been an anchor all my life.

I will always remember the warm welcome I received from the wives of my former teachers, Eunike Semugoma, Elsie Kizito and Dalison Biriba, when I returned to Budo. Their love and care created a bond of friendship between us that lasted until they all passed on about thirty, forty years later.

I settled in as a teacher's wife and homemaker in a community where practically everyone knew me.

Spiritually, I found myself back in the revival atmosphere of the *Balokole* community. There was a oneness amongst a few staff, students and neighbourhood residents who participated in the regular Sunday fellowships at the school. On my part, the wives in the fellowship, especially Gladys Sebbowa, supported me with a lot of love.

Later that year, this oneness opened a door for me to attend an evangelistic convention at Kako Church, eighty-five miles west of Kampala. The convention was led by pioneers from the East African Revival Movement at Gahini, Rwanda, including Dr Joe Church. I was, perhaps, among the youngest at that gathering but I did not feel the age difference. The convention spurred a big leap in my spiritual growth.

Barely a year after our wedding, I became a mother. Our first child, a daughter, Elizabeth Erusa Kirabo Nakalema, arrived on 23rd November 1950. Katie Kibuka was one of the first people to visit me at Mulago Hospital when Betty was born and I remember how she sweetly remarked, "Rhoda, you will now have someone to call you *Maama*." She was one of Betty's godparents and she continued to be a key person in my married life. Being a teacher and a mother of four, she was my adviser in many ways, and she gave me special tips on bringing up children. Her youngest child, Christine, was five months younger than Betty, and the two grew to be very close. They even attended the same primary school. Her two sons, Sam and Robin, were close to my sons, William and Peter, and they all went to the same primary and secondary schools.

In our second year of marriage, just as I was getting used to motherhood, a vacancy opened up at Budo. The school needed a part-time teacher in the commercial course department. This was timely, because a second child was on the way and we needed to supplement William's income. We decided that I take up the offer and inevitably, I had to get a nanny to take care of baby Nakalema. Nanyonga, the nanny we employed, was a lovely young girl who had, unfortunately, missed out on schooling. She loved my daughter and gave her a good start.

On 17th January 1952, our second child, William Samson Kalema or William Jnr arrived. We named him William after his father, and Samson after his paternal grandfather. His father was very excited that he now had a son who would join the fight against the South African apartheid system that angered him greatly. The younger William, however, never developed any interest in political activism.

Visit to My In-laws Home in Kiboga

When I got married to William, I realised that he loved his birthplace and roots deeply and I had no alternative but to embrace Kiboga as my home. I grew to love the place and the people and for most of my life, Kiboga has been a part of me. It is a relationship that started off on a low level but became deep and special with the years.

I did not visit William's parents' home before our marriage. Whereas his mother and family attended our wedding, sadly, William's father did not as he had lost his eyesight a few months before our wedding. Therefore, he never saw me. William told me that his father lamented this until his death twelve years later, in 1962. My first visit to Kiboga was in April 1952, two years after we got married. I travelled without William. At the time, he was the secretary of the Uganda Teachers' Association and he was scheduled to attend the annual teachers' conference. I took along our two babies, Betty who was about one-and-half-years old, and three-month-old William Jr. My sister-in-law, Mary Nakiyimba, accompanied me to help with the babies. It was a happy two-week visit. The children and I were excitedly and wholeheartedly embraced by our new family and by all my husband's relatives, especially by William's elder sisters, Erivania and Kasalina, and his elder brother, Katerega. In later years, we visited with William more regularly as the children grew older and our family became bigger. We made Kiboga our family home.

* * *

In September of the following year, 1953, William left for Edinburgh University in Scotland to study for a degree. This had always been his great desire but at the time, Makerere College did not offer any degree courses. With William away, I could not continue at Budo as a part-time teacher. So, I applied for a full-time job as a bursar-secretary at Buloba Teacher Training College. Buloba, a missionary-founded college, was close to Budo and I enjoyed my job and its homely atmosphere. It suited me and my two toddlers, and I had a third one on the way.

On 24th April 1954, our son, Peter Martin Kayondo was born. The children, particularly the new baby, were adored by the students and staff, especially by Miss Ethel Parker the college principal. When Martin was six months old, I invited Bishop Leslie Brown to Buloba to baptise him. Rt. Reverend Leslie Brown and his wife, Winifred Brown, came to Uganda in March 1953 with their daughter, Alison, when Reverend Brown succeeded Bishop Cyril Simon Stuart as Bishop of Uganda. When they arrived, our family was still at Budo.

By the beginning of 1954, the Browns and I were friends and the Bishop willingly accepted my request. He performed the baptism at the historical Buloba village church – St Stephens of Kasero. Bishop Brown became very attached to baby Peter and he would often ask, "How is my baby?" He later became the Archbishop of Uganda, Rwanda and Burundi. Mrs Brown became my mentor and friend until she died in October 1999, in England.

I shall always remember the serious health challenges that I faced with the children in the two years before I joined William in the United Kingdom in September 1955. Halfway through our stay in Buloba, William Jnr, then aged two, had a frightful malaria attack. It developed fast, and the high fever brought on convulsions in the middle of the night. At that time, all I could do was pray. I had to wait until morning when we could get a ride to the hospital in the school van.

On another occasion, a furious attack of whooping cough overwhelmed him and his sister, Betty. The bouts of coughing from deep within the chest would make them double over and leave them exhausted. The school stepped in again and I got the children to hospital in Kampala fairly quickly in the school van. By then, immunisation against childhood diseases was unknown in the country. When we arrived at Mulago Hospital, I was informed that the children needed immediate treatment otherwise the illness would linger for up to six weeks. I got the money for the first dose of medication from my cousin, Dr John Kasirye and before long, the children recovered.

* * *

After two years at Buloba, we decided that I should take advantage of a government scholarship that was offered to wives of students and join William in Edinburgh. I resigned from my job at Buloba and although I was leaving my young children with our immediate loving family, it was still a hard decision to make. William's sister, Erivania, a midwife, and her husband, Erisa Mugenyi, a teacher, had two children of their own, Eleanor and Ben. They gladly took in our two older children who were close in age to their children, while my mother took in Peter Martin, who was sixteen months old.

In addition to the scholarship, the government offered students who were studying abroad a stipend and this is the money that helped care for the children in our absence.

Chapter 6

Further Studies in the United Kingdom

As I boarded the plane at Entebbe Airport in September 1955 and waved farewell to my children and family, I was aware that I was entering a new phase of life.

I recall the joy I felt when I saw William who had travelled from Edinburgh by train to meet me. We spent three days in London and during that time, he took me sightseeing. We visited historical and monumental sites including Buckingham Palace, Westminster Abbey and the Houses of Parliament. Before leaving for Edinburgh, we also visited Uganda House that housed the student advisor's office and Mutesa House near Hyde Park. The latter, a popular place for Baganda students, was the property of the Kabaka's government.

My first impression of Edinburgh was that it was a solidly built, beautiful, old city. I learnt that some sections of the city were hundreds of years old and that the modern parts were merged with the old, so one could walk on a street with stone pavings that were centuries old and enter a modern shop that was only a few decades old. Edinburgh Castle, set on a hilltop overlooking the Princes Street Gardens and Princes Street, was the most historic feature in the city.

At the time, Edinburgh was one of the cities in Scotland with trams for urban transport – which I found fascinating. They were operated by the Edinburgh Corporation Tramways; the last tram was phased out in my last year there. The trams were small bus-like passenger coaches that ran on rails, with electric cables hanging above them. Revived interest in trams in Scotland towards the end of the 20th Century, led to their re-introduction.

The Scottish accent was markedly different from the English one and William informed me that it was because their traditional language was Gaelic. I had difficulty understanding them at first. Despite that, the people were very friendly.

We made many friends and I settled down and loved Scotland. I realised, for the first time, that the United Kingdom had a variety of inhabitants – the English, Scots, Welsh and Irish. I learnt that the Scots were extremely good at crafting things with their hands and so they were good as mechanics, carpenters, stonemasons, and builders. In fact, Ugandans owe a great debt to this Scottish craftsmanship. According to history, most of Uganda's technical education and therefore the physical building of modern Uganda, was founded on Scottish missionary Alexander Mackay's (October 1849 – February 1890) training. His technical brilliance amazed the Baganda who flocked to his workshop daily. Every time he demonstrated another breakthrough, such as pumping water out of apparently nowhere, they would exclaim, *"Makayi lubaale ddala!"* (Mackay is a god indeed!).

* * *

Before I left Uganda, arrangements were made for me to join the Newbattle Abbey College, an adult education institution in East Lothian, just outside Edinburgh. I was enrolled for a one year preliminary bridging course in General Social Studies, that would close the gap between my 'ordinary' level stage of education that I attained at Budo in 1947, and any further studies that I chose to pursue. It was not yet clear what I would do after the one year was over, as William would still have another year of study remaining.

The college was housed in a former Abbey – a massive structure on a large acreage that characterised the past life of the aristocracy. All the students were adults and the majority were Scots. There were two English, one Norwegian (Sonia), one American (Judith Hines) and two Ugandans, Crispin Kisosonkole and I. My roommate was Jean McLean who was about forty years older than me. We all became friends and it was particularly difficult when it came to saying the final farewells at the end of the year. I always remember how when it came to Sonia the Norwegian, I said: "Sonia, I think we may not meet again, except perhaps in heaven." She replied frantically, with eyes wide open, "But Rhoda, I do not believe in that."

Overall, I enjoyed my studies, particularly the psychology class that was taught by Mr Gordon. Although this was an entirely new subject for me, it sensitised me, gave meaning to many aspects of life and prepared me for the university course that I would later take at Edinburgh University.

Social Studies at Edinburgh University

Towards the end of the 1955/1956 academic year, the Newbattle Abbey College recommended that I get admitted to Edinburgh University for a certificate course in Social Studies. I happily took up the course, especially because I was going to join William in his final year. Since the original government financial assistance only covered one year, I needed more funds. Fortunately, encouraged by my tutor's reports, Mr L. A. Mathias, the Uganda students' advisor in London, who always had goodwill toward Ugandan students, recommended that the government extend my scholarship for another two years. In October 1956, I started the certificate course at Edinburgh University together with a few other students from my former college, Newbattle Abbey.

I found the course extremely interesting, especially social biology (the study of body functions and behaviour) and anthropology (the study of 'primitive' societies). These courses proved to be useful later when I sought to understand the roots of poverty and other social problems in the different communities in Uganda. I was astonished, but my tutor did not seem surprised, when I scored the top mark of 72 per cent in the anthropology exam. I thought that perhaps he thought that I was studying my natural environment, and therefore, I was 'at home' with the subject. I remember two tutors whose teaching left a lasting impression – Dr McGreggor, a soft-spoken lady tutor, who made learning enjoyable, and the head of the Social Studies Department, Miss Marjorie Brown, who was always neatly dressed, kind and calm. We hosted Miss Brown at our home in Uganda in 1959 when she visited Makerere University College.

We also took some courses alongside students who were studying for their degrees. The classes in political economy, economic history and psychology were eye-openers and I took a renewed interest in these subjects and topics that William had always spoken passionately about. Matters of national importance to which I had paid no attention before, became clear.

Although, during this time, William was in his final year and working very hard, he always readily helped me with my essays on economic history and political economy – the subjects that he too was studying. He was very determined to help improve my education and make my time in Edinburgh as worthwhile as possible. This is an endowment from him that I have lived with all my life. During his last year, and my first, at university, we lived in 'digs' – student accommodation – at 173 Bruntsfield Crescent, a homely environment in the house of Mrs Sarah Browning.

We were members of the African Students Union of Edinburgh University that visited Wales during the Christmas season of 1956. The week-long visit was organised by the chaplain of the students' union, Reverend Robin Barbour. We were hosted with great humour and charm, and I especially remember one dinner party where the Welsh, who have a language that hardly has any vowels, pointed out the characteristics of the different British nationalities.

Some of the banter included, "The English believe they made the world and they worship the Creator."

"The Scottish," we were told, "keep the Sabbath very strictly, as they keep everything else, especially their money." (It is true that the Scottish were very particular about keeping Sunday holy and I remember that night clubs in all the towns in Scotland were closed by midnight on Saturday nights).

"The Irish believe in nothing and can fight about anything."

"A Welshman from Cardiganshire can buy something from a Jew, sell it to a Scotsman and still make a profit", they joked. One needed to know about the hard bargains that Jews drive and the reputed tight fistedness of Scotsmen, in order to appreciate the superiority of Cardiganshire Welshmen here.

On what turned out to be a very entertaining evening, we were also told the story about how the Welsh Bible survived. In the late 1800s, we were informed, Queen Victoria, desiring to make all of Britain Anglican, wanted the Welsh to read the English Bible and to also speak English. The Welsh cunningly told the Queen, "Your Majesty, the Welsh people would love to become Anglican and read the Bible. However, they are likely to understand it much better if they read it in Welsh." The Queen gave in and they kept their Welsh Bible. It is little wonder that in 1904, the great historic Welsh Revival, led by Evan Roberts, broke out.

William was awarded a Master of Arts (Hons) degree in Economics in July 1957 when he graduated. He subsequently returned home to our children, leaving me behind, to complete my studies. It was sad seeing him off but I was consoled by the thought that he was returning to our children.

It was around this time that I visited Nancy Corby, who had retired in 1950 as the headmistress of Gayaza High School. She had also resigned from the CMS in 1953 and retreated to her home in Somerset. We continued to communicate through letters and Christmas cards until 1988, when she passed away.

* * *

I had good friends during my time at Edinburgh University who were a great comfort after William left. Among the friends was Florence Biddy Russell, who, even after leaving Edinburgh, continued sending me Scottish calendars every Christmas for fifty years, until she passed away in 2006. Another was Beryl Knotts who went to live in Oxford and whom I met a number of times in London and at her home in Oxford. I value the annual newsletters which she still sends. She gave me a present of two beautiful, hand-painted cups in 2006.

Jill Jordan, Mary Kneal and Judith Hines made my life very comfortable, happy and secure. With this team of mature friends – some 'very mature' – we proved that age was just a number. Ours was a group full of spirit and fun, in and out of college. This international team made me realise the beauty of global friendships. I started to think like a 'global citizen', able to put myself in the shoes of a person halfway across the world, because I could feel their humanity. I knew they were like me; able to cry and laugh and miss their families. Then, to top it all, there was Professor Arnold and Mary Klopper, a God-sent couple.

When William arrived in Britain in September 1953, he already strongly opposed the apartheid political system in South Africa. In London, he met Mary Klopper, who together with her husband Arnold, had left South Africa following the implementation of the apartheid laws by the Nationalist Party in 1948. Mary was, at the time, the political assistant to Fenner Brockway, a renowned anti-colonialist British Labour MP. She had already linked up with two other fierce Ugandan critics of the South Africa apartheid system, Ignatius Musaazi and Abu Mayanja, who were known to William. The common cause cemented the friendship of the three Ugandans and Mary and this enhanced their political activism. For a long time afterwards, Mary Klopper had three 'brothers' from Uganda – Ignatius Musaazi, Abu Mayanja, and William Kalema.

In 1952, Ignatius Musaazi had formed the Uganda National Congress, the first political party in Uganda. He was its first president and Abu Mayanja was its first secretary-general. The party laid a foundation for the political activities that eventually led to independence.

About a year later, the Kloppers moved to Edinburgh. By the time I joined William in 1955, they were among the three couples who were his good friends; the others were David and Eileen Michie, and John and Eileen Spencer.

Later, they moved to Aberdeen where Arnold taught at the medical school at Aberdeen University. In the late 1960s, we started exchanging Christmas greetings and our friendship was renewed. Our friendship with Mary and Arnold Klopper was to prove an asset to us, especially in regards to the overseas studies that various members of my family undertook. The couple's kindness was manifested on many occasions in the years that followed.

* * *

In addition to the academic course, I carried out two practical assignments during the summer holidays of 1957. First, I spent two weeks at the Tynepark Approved School for girls in Scotland. What stood out most for me were the number of teenage girls from 'one-parent' families. It was not uncommon then for fathers to run away from home, some exiling themselves as far away as Eastern Europe. Most of the girls were very bitter. One morning, as I was teaching the girls how to make their beds, I said to one of them jokingly, "Margo, you must learn to make a bed so you can make your husband's bed when you get married." She responded with great anger: "Mrs Kalema, I will never get married, but if I do, I will kill my husband". Her father had abandoned her and her mother when she was very young.

Next, I worked for three weeks under a Miss Ogilvy, in a probation office in Lancaster where I had to deal with children of working-class families. Lancaster was a linoleum industrial city and many parents had little education. I will always remember Ms Ogilvy's remarks on her report about my practical work. "This student," she wrote, "has a lot of common sense." It was then that I realised, common sense was not so common, after all.

During the Easter holidays of 1958, I spent three weeks at a children's social welfare office in East London on attachment. This office was mainly engaged in caring for 'Children in Need of Care and Protection' and 'Children out of Control'. At this office, I faced the reality of truancy – children running away from home and skipping school. The ultimate cause of delinquency, I observed, was the disorganisation and disengagement of the parents with little parental love, or love for each other. The children came from 'homes with no calendar or clock' – homes without order or systems.

In my last year (1957-58), I moved into a student residence, Playfair Hall, which was a bus ride away from college. In July 1958, I completed the course successfully and was among fifteen students who were awarded a Certificate in Social Studies.

As the end of our time together approached, our group took the opportunity to visit different sites in Edinburgh, places that we would probably never find the time to visit again. We went to Arthur's Seat, a flat historical hill in Edinburgh, Edinburgh Castle, and Holyrood Palace. Then it was time to set off for our various homes.

We kept in touch for many years from our various corners of the world. Our experiences had changed us and we all got something that was extra precious from our time together – friendship.

Before returning home, my new focus on social and political issues was enhanced by the opportunity I got to attend the International Union of Child Welfare Congress in Brussels, Belgium, from the 20th to 26th of July, 1958. The theme was, "The Parents' Role in Child Development." Mrs Winifred Brown's encouragement and support once again came into play. She urged me to attend the congress and the student advisor at Uganda House, Mr Mathias, made it possible for me to get the required funds. The congress' emphasis was on studying the needs of children and it gave participants a global perspective. For me, it enhanced the knowledge I had acquired at my Edinburgh course and it was very timely, as the offer came just before I headed home, where I was going to put into practice what I had learnt about child development. The course of my life was already changing, and I was headed into a new field, people development, and politics.

Immediately after the conference in Belgium, I returned home to a wildly joyful welcome from my three children, husband, mother and many members of my wider family. The Kalema family was re-united and we settled down to start a new phase of life.

Chapter 7

Civil Service

When I returned home, the children were three years older. Betty was seven-and-a-half, William Jnr six-and-a-half and Peter Martin four. William had been alone with them for a year. We rented a small house on Namirembe Hill. Since Betty and William Jnr were already in boarding school at King's College Budo Junior School, we only had Peter at home. On his return, William had been employed by the American Embassy. His stay was short-lived though, because before long, he was appointed Assistant Permanent Secretary in the Education Ministry in the Buganda Government. According to him, he enjoyed the latter job more because education was his passion, main field of study, and experience.

Probation and Social Welfare Department

After settling down, it became necessary that I introduce myself to the Social and Community Development Ministry, the government's arm that was relevant to my training. Obtaining a job was not easy at first because the government had never recruited a social worker with the level of a British – or any other – university training. In the ministry at the time, Harriet Kawalya Kagwa, my former schoolmate at Budo, had the highest training in the field. She had attended a prestigious college in South Africa where she studied social work.

The other few Ugandan officers in the ministry were basically administrators in the colonial government and a few other employees were 'learning on the job' (in-service training). Also, up to about 1957, as the ministry's title suggests, it focused on developing communities and improving the lives of people in villages by offering informal education and conducting adult literacy classes for men and women.

At the time, many social problems now common in urban areas had not seriously emerged in Kampala or any other urban centres in the country. Nevertheless, the police and courts were already experiencing problems with children. A Probation and Social Welfare Office and a Remand Home in Kampala were, therefore, established to handle children involved in court cases. The Approved School at Kampiringisa had already been established for young people who would otherwise have been sent to prison. My training was geared towards this latter group. However, I also worked with non-governmental organisations like the Sanyu Babies' Home, Save the Children Fund and the Catholic Adoption Society that took in and placed orphaned and abandoned babies.

As early as 1952, the government had already established a training centre called the Nsamizi Training Institute in Entebbe. It enrolled 'O' level students for nine to twelve months training in various courses including Social Welfare and Community Development. After training, they were posted to the ministry and were very effective in the probation and social welfare office. The institute was managed jointly by the same Social and Community Development Ministry and Makerere College.

My appointment finally came through in September 1958, when I joined the Ministry as a Community Development

Officer. This was per the Standing Orders of the Civil Service, but my work was that of a Probation and Welfare Officer. In 1959, I was confirmed in the same position and I was also given more responsibilities. As time went on, it was evident that my training and experience became increasingly relevant, even though the circumstances and nature of social problems in Britain and Uganda varied tremendously.

Together with my fellow staff who had trained at Nsamizi Institute, we made a good team. We discussed the very difficult and interesting cases and worked together on writing case reports and recommendations to the Juvenile Court. We noted that many serious cases were the result of parental negligence. In one case, a child who was picked up by the police in town told us that his father was dead. When we arrived at his home village, we found out that the father was alive. He was asked to report to court on a certain date and he did. Our report stated that the father was dead because that was what the child told us. The Judge, after looking at the report and the father, asked him a few questions. The Judge, saddened by the father's answers and behaviour, told him, "Indeed, your son was right; you are dead."

Another case involved a mother who had nine children. Her husband had exiled himself to America, but she had remained close to her mother-in-law. Although the father sent funds for their education, she lost interest in her children and abandoned them in a house close to their grandmother's home. When we got hold of her on account of her children running wild and stealing, she came to the office and told us, "I cannot be bothered with the children anymore. I did my duty. I bled nine times."

The Probation and Welfare Department was mostly involved in the handling of children who were in "need of care and protection" because they were deserted or had no parents. It also provided for babies that were abandoned at birth and lost children. The department came across many cases of lost children aged between six and thirteen, who left their homes to visit relatives in towns but failed to find them. The cases were often painful and challenging, but also interesting. It was always very rewarding when a child was reunited with the parents or relatives, or when an abandoned infant who was placed in an orphanage grew up into an active member of the community.

Juveniles who were 'out-of-control' and got involved in criminal activities, often innocently, were some of the painful cases that our office handled. After they were placed in remand homes, we would present them in court and go to their homes which were, more often than not, in distant villages. This would mean a day's journey – to and fro. The directions were sometimes vague, as would be the names of the parents because the frightened children were the only source of information. Some gave parents' names as 'Maama', 'Taata', or '*Mukyala* (Ms) Nalubega'. In such cases, local administrators – chiefs at all levels – would provide us with more detailed information about the family, why and how 'our case' was found in the city centre. Often the reason would be unfavourable circumstances at home, in particular the negative attitudes of parents (or step-parents) and mothers who abandoned their homes.

The case of a little girl of five who was found lost at the main bus park in Kampala is embedded in my mind. When she was asked where she came from and how she got there, she answered, "I came with *Maama*". Asked why they had left home, she responded in Luganda: "*Twajja kunoba*. (We deserted home)". It was sad to hear that. It was as if she, too, had been involved in her mother's decision. She was eventually reunited with her mother after we took her to a police station.

Apart from the office and fieldwork, which engaged me fully, I lectured students at Nsamizi Training Institute. Since the institute also had agriculture and veterinary students, I suggested that we could share information on the social needs and problems that we came across with the students who would eventually work within the same communities we worked in around the country. As the officer in charge, I also played a role in healing family breakdowns, including reconciling husbands and wives, for the sake of the children. I was greatly satisfied by two families that turned out to be the happiest after our intervention. Both mothers had made up their minds to leave their husbands. One of the two mothers was pregnant when she came to the office. I succeeded in persuading the mothers not to abandon their homes. Their children grew up to be well-balanced men and women, got married and became useful members of society. Their families and mine became friends. Many years later, I attended the wedding of one of the ladies' grandchildren.

One of these families had two daughters, Juliet and Betty Tamusuza, who settled in Atlanta, Georgia. I met them when I visited my son, William, in Delaware in 1988. The opportunity presented itself when I was invited by my American friends, Dr and Mrs Al and Pat Rhea to their home and to attend a Christian convention in Atlanta. When I met the girls, it was about twenty-four years after I had met and worked with their mother. The two girls attended the same church as the Rheas and when they heard that I was around, they invited me to their home. They took me to important sites around the city, including the Martin Luther King Centre and the Stone Mountain. They finally gave me a parting gift of some lovely fabric. I was accorded the same good care as their parents who often visited them for vacations and for medical care.

In the course of my work, I also attended a week-long Child Welfare Conference in Accra, Ghana, in December 1960. When visiting a village there, as part of the conference's programme, I found out that Ghana, which had gained independence barely three years earlier, had more advanced social welfare services in their rural areas as well as in their urban centres. I noted this in my report to the Ministry. As a result, by 1964, Uganda, too had improved community programmes for women and children that focused on uplifting their livelihoods.

* * *

Although the office had government vehicles and drivers who transported staff, William gave me driving lessons on some afternoons after work. Later, I went for five professional lessons at the Alex Driving School and I easily passed the test. I got my driving permit on 31st July 1959. Later, I acquired a small car, a two-door Fiat, for 600 shillings on hire purchase, and it made moving around easier.

One day, I had an accident while returning from Kampiringisa Approved School, twenty-five miles off the Kampala-Masaka Road. The car wheels slid on loose gravel and the car ended up facing the direction I had come from. The side mirror cut me on the temple. I was considerably shaken but luckily, I was near the school and help arrived quickly.

* * *

Just before the country's independence in early 1962, there was serious consideration about me taking over from the topmost Senior Community Development Officer, a European lady called Ms Antoinette Swart. At the same time, I was appointed Community Development Officer in Mbale, (Eastern Uganda). This latter appointment proved hard for me to accept because there was no way I was going to leave my family and move so far away, so I resigned. I remember how my husband and my brother, Kiwana, were annoyed by the Ministry's decision. My brother wrote a short article in the *Uganda Argus* newspaper protesting my unfair transfer. After about two months, I was recalled and appointed officer in charge of the Probation and Welfare Department. I replaced Mr Herbert who left soon after and returned to England.

Building a Home in Muyenga

William was keen on establishing a home of our own. He bought a one-acre piece of land on Muyenga Hill, also known as Tank Hill, from a landowner called Mr Etuusa. He reasoned that since it looked like his future work would be centred around Kampala, we needed to build a house in the city. At the time, the western side of the hill was sparsely populated, very bushy and was mosquito infested. It later became a popular, upscale suburb.

I have always been intrigued by how we put up our first house with meagre resources. When we started building in November 1958, we had many challenges that had to be overcome simultaneously. The first was the mosquito hazard that required that we fix wire mesh to all the windows to keep them out and which meant an additional expense.

My Father, Katikiro Martin Luther Nsibirwa

My mother,
Veronica
Namuddu

Katikiro Nsibirwa with his wife Mukubwa and members of his
household. Children Sara and Rhoda seated 3rd and 4th from left, 1938

Sir Apolo Kagwa,
Katikiro of Buganda,
1890 – 1926

Temutewo Mulondo,
Father's maternal
uncle

Kabaka Edward Mutesa II standing between Katikiro Nsibirwa (right)
and Omuwanika Lauri Kiwanuka. Dennis Herbert, Headmaster of
Kings College Budo is behind the boy on the right, 1940

Katikiro Martin Luther Nsibirwa receiving the Damula, the instrument
of power, July 7th 1945

Kings College Budo, Primary 6 Girls. L-R: Rhoda Bamutyakoki, Rhoda Nsibirwa, Edith Stokes, Mary Stokes, Bitijuma Sekagya and Edisa Sendikwanawa, 1941

Commercial class at Kings College Budo with Mr Hillier, 1947

Our wedding day, February 11th 1950

Katie Kironde and Janet Nsibirwa, Buloba, early 1940's

Rhoda with oldest three children, 1955

With the graduating class of social studies, Edinburgh University,
July 1958

In front of the Palace of Canongate, Edinburgh Holyroodhouse.
L-R: Beryl Knotts, Rhoda Kalema and Isobel Forgan, 1958

Kiwana, Rhoda and William, Edinburgh, 1956

Rhoda and William at William's graduation, McEwan Hall,
Edinburgh, 1957

Duke and Duchess of Kent visiting Lubiri, October 1962.
L-R: Mr Musisi, Rhoda, Duke and Duchess, Eriver Kigundu

HRH Princess Margaret planting a tree at Tororo Girls' School,
March 1965. I am standing at the back wearing a white hat

Uganda Council of Women. Front row 4th from right is Edith Bataringaya, next to her is Sugra Visram, centre is Miria Obote, and Rhoda Kalema 4th from left, 1960s

First female students at Makerere College, 1945. Seated: Mary Senkatuka, Margaret Mulyanti Standing: L-R Florence Wamala, Catherine Senkatuka, Marjorie Kamuhigi, Jemima Ntungwerisho

Rhoda Kalema and Rebecca Mulira with Minister for Education, Dr Joshua Luyimbazi Zake and a ministry staff at the UNESCO Conference, November 1962

Uganda's winning hockey team on return from New Delhi. Front row. L-R: Mr Sandhu (Team leader), Mr Anywar, Rhoda Kalema, Freda Lule (Assistant Captain), C. B. Katiti (Minister of Culture & Community Development), S. W. Kulubya (Mayor of Kampala), Harjeet Sandhu (Team Captain), Miriam Sozi (Team leader), 1968

Rhoda & William, at the Empire State Building, New York, 1967

With William as Minister for Works and Communications and Zac Kaheru at the commissioning of 'Umoja' Steamer at Mwanza, Lake Victoria, 1967

Seated L-R: Rhoda, Katerega, William Snr, Nakibule and Betty.
Standing L-R: Peter Martin, William Jnr, 1967

The family with the new addition, baby Gladys Nalubowa, 1970

Commonwealth Parliamentary Association. Centre is President Obote (with stick), left of him is Chief Justice Udo Udoma, 4th left is Speaker of Parliament Narendra Patel, William and Rhoda Kalema right of President Obote, 1967

The second challenge was getting water, electricity and a telephone line to the house. These were real hurdles at the end of 1958 because ours was a lone house on a hill with no close neighbours and the only way up to the site was a footpath. This was widened by trucks as they ferried building materials up the hill. We applied to the Uganda Electricity Board and Uganda Posts and Telecommunications for services. In each case, we had to pay for every pole that was required to reach the nearest power and telephone connections. When it came to water, the huge pipes that supplied Kampala City and beyond were highly pressurised and so although they passed very close to our house, tapping water from them was out of the question. We were advised to buy pipes that would cover the distance – over a thousand metres – from a connection at the site to the main tanks, on top of the hill. We succeeded in getting water to the site and for some time, we collected it for home use from the back yard until we fitted internal plumbing.

The move into our new home on 24th April 1959 coincided with our son, Peter Martin's fifth birthday. However, soon after settling down, we started seeing snakes around the home. Combating snakes in the midst of a virgin bush is very difficult and one sad result was the loss of our black Labrador to a snake bite. We were grateful that despite the children and their cousins playing around the grounds, until we moved out in 1966, the dog was their only victim.

About six months after we moved in, we succeeded in getting all the amenities installed and for the next seven years, we enjoyed living there and hosting our family members and friends. Our first five children spent their early childhood there. The house, with its 'small red roof' within a wide green bush, was very noticeable from many places around Kampala and it attracted many people who scrambled for the land around us.

We moved to the city centre in 1966 so we could commute more easily to our places of work. By then, the original footpath up the hill had become a real road leading to several lovely homes. Many years later, we requested the local authorities that the former footpath be named in memory of its pioneer and they agreed. In January 1997, it was officially named William W. Kalema Drive. After almost sixty years, Muyenga Hill is no longer a green hill near Kampala, it has become a fully developed, affluent city suburb.

* * *

The time came when family demands increased because not only was my husband heavily engaged in government duties, the family had also increased in number since 1960. The situation was compounded by health problems that weighed me down and I finally retired in mid 1966.

When I left the civil service, the department was all set for the future. Our office had a good number of dedicated and efficient staff. Robinah Nakabugo, Marjorie Nsereko, and Veronica Kiddu, the Probation and Welfare Assistants, were good with young girls. I found Nathan Kintu in the office when I joined and although he was much older, he was full of enthusiasm. Blasio Kiyaga was also older and very committed, as was John Lutaya. They were all officers. There was also James Senkaaba, who was a clerk and record keeper. New branches were opened in Jinja, Mbale, and Masaka.

Chapter 8

Joining the Women's Movement

My decision to join the women's movement was greatly influenced by Dr Winifred Brown, the wife of the Bishop of Uganda, Reverend Leslie Brown. Although I was not aware of it then, looking back, she must have seen something in me as she drew me close to her and mentored me. Even as I prepared to proceed for further studies in 1955, she lent me journals from India where she and her husband had served before coming to Uganda. The journals had articles that illustrated how ignorance among women affected family and community life in India. Looking through the journals, I realised that although she was a medical doctor, her heart was set on improving the social wellbeing of women and children.

Soon after I arrived from Edinburgh University in 1958, she encouraged me to join a crusade that she was heading within the Uganda Council of Women (UCW) which was involved in fighting for women's rights and social justice. My decision to join the women's movement was not easy. I had just been appointed Community Development and Probation Officer in Kampala, a full-time job. Moreover, UCW committee meetings usually lasted until 6.00 p.m. and this meant that my three young children, who had just rediscovered me, were once again going to miss my attention. All the same, I joined the UCW and the Uganda Association of University Women (UAUW). The former was to engage a substantial part of my life.

The UCW had evolved from the Women's League in 1946 and when I joined, it consisted of European, African and Asian women. In a rapidly changing post World War II Uganda that was headed for independence, women wanted an organisation that would bring together women from different races, religions and backgrounds to take up and influence issues including public opinion and the government policies that affected them. Among the organisations' prominent members were Eseza Makumbi, Barbara Saben, Catherine Hastie, Sugra Visram, Maherah Ahmad, and Hemantini Bhatia. Before long, UCW became a foundation for the women's movement and it even reached out to uneducated and rural women by forming links with community development clubs throughout the country.

Getting Governor Sir Andrew Cohen to appoint African women to the Legislative Council (LegCo) was one of UCW's first achievements. That is how, in 1956 Pumla Kisonsonkole became the first African woman representative at the LegCo, followed by Sarah Nyendwoha Ntiro, Joyce Masembe Mpanga and Frances Akello in 1958. Later these women would use this platform to argue strongly for women to vote in the elections before independence

UCW took on various activities. Training featured prominently as the organisation sought to promote the training of nursery school teachers, lobbied for the training of girls and women in homemaking, cookery, handcrafts and needlework and offered language classes – English for Africans and Asians, and Luganda for European women. UCW was instrumental in the creation of the School for the Deaf at Namirembe.

The need for low income housing was also addressed. The UCW successfully appealed to the government to build houses for low-income earners at Naguru and to construct centres that would accommodate women when they attended conferences. It initiated a women's magazine, *Nyabo,* and other print media including a women's page that was introduced in the *Uganda Argus*, the main English-language newspaper and in 1956, in the Luganda language weekly, *Uganda Empya.*[5]

One of the most lasting outcomes of the UCW activities was the setting up of the Young Women's Christian Association (YWCA) in Uganda. This was after the organisation requested the YWCA in the USA to start a Uganda chapter and Miss Sue Steel, an American, was seconded to Uganda. In 1952, two Ugandan women, Katie Kibuka and Rebecca Mulira, underwent nine months of training in the USA and on their return, the YWCA was firmly established and has remained active since then.

The UCW initiated numerous legislative changes that would positively impact on the status of women. In December 1958, during the UCW Annual General Meeting, Eseza Makumbi moved a resolution that would introduce a legislation that declared, "All marriages should be registered." It was unanimously passed and it covered all marriages, be they civil, religious or customary. UCW created a special sub-committee called the Sub-Committee on the Status of Women, which comprised of Winifred Brown, Barbara Saben, Sarah Ntiro, Eseza Makumbi and later, I, as the secretary. Being

---

5   Aili Mari Tripp, *Women and Politics in Uganda* (Madison: University of Wisconsin Press, 2000), p. 38.

the youngest in the group, I was eager to learn from these intelligent and dedicated women. Little did I know that I was taking my first steps into the struggle for women's justice and that the assignment would endow me with a useful lifetime experience. I learnt from them that I have to speak up for what I believe in.

In 1957 and 1959, the Sub-committee sent out two questionnaires to all women's organisations including the Anglican Mothers' Union and the Catholic Women's Club. The government's community development clubs that were operated by the Ministry of Community Development around the country were also sampled. The questionnaires covered marriage, divorce, inheritance and the status of women. Issues such as the Right to Work, Making Wills, Bride Price and Maternity Leave for African Women in the civil service were also included.

By early 1960, we received many enthusiastic, revealing responses which indicated that our cause was timely. The activity also coincided with a countrywide awakening among women, church leaders, and the government. For instance, women in northern Uganda had already reported to Barbara Saben and members of the LegCo about the mistreatment by husbands, a situation that was condoned and compounded by cultural traditions in certain areas.

In March 1960, the UCW organised a conference on the Status of Women, the first of its kind in Uganda – headed by the Sub-Committee on the Status of Women. The conference was held at the National Theatre in Kampala and was very well attended by representatives from all over the country. It was non-tribal, non-racial, non-religious and all inclusive. Regardless of their status in society, women participated enthusiastically led by experts on issues like bride price, property inheritance, rights of succession, marriage laws, women in public life, the right of wives to work, and maternity leave. The event was widely covered in the print media and on radio and was a great success.

The conference made several significant resolutions, the main ones being that all marriages should be registered; the return of bride price upon separation be abolished; people should be educated on writing wills; a widow (with or without children) should receive a substantial share of her husband's property; wives would be allowed to go out to work for gain and, working women should be granted maternity leave. Thus, while the country was demanding political independence and preparing for the first internal self-government elections, women, through the UCW Sub-committee, were demanding recognition and social justice.

The prevailing atmosphere in the country helped both genders appreciate the work of the UCW. This also made it easier to educate and mobilise women's groups for the general elections of 1962. It is important to note that a number of the resolutions required political will and leadership. Leaders needed to educate society for it to realise the necessity for change when it came to some cultural practises.

The resolution to grant maternity leave to Ugandan mothers in the public service was finally sanctioned by the government in 1968. During the conference preparations, I was expecting our fourth child. Therefore, although I personally did not benefit from the maternity leave resolution, I got much satisfaction from the fact that I played a part in bringing about justice and comfort to working Ugandan mothers.

Another important outcome of the conference was the resolution that the existing laws on marriage in Uganda be translated into different languages and published in booklets. The UCW Sub-committee embarked on this work in 1961 and English, Luganda, Luo, Runyoro-Rutoro, Runyankole-Rukiga and Iteso copies were published and sold through women's organisations at one shilling and fifty cents each. Men also bought the book.

Pushing Women Issues in the New Government

As independence drew near, the Uganda Association of University Women (UAUW), linked up with UCW from 1961 to 1962 to prepare women for the parliamentary elections. UAUW was established by Mary Stuart, the wife of the Bishop of Uganda, Rt Reverend Cyril Stuart, to address the low enrolment of women in university. A university graduate, as were her four sisters, Mary Stuart advocated for the enrolment of females, including older women, at the Makerere College. That is how five female teachers, Mary Senkatuka, Florence Wamala, Jemima Ntungwerisho, Marjorie Kamuhigi and Margaret Mulyanti, educated at historic girls schools and the Buloba Teacher Training College, and a 'fresh' Catherine Senkatuka from Kings College Budo, were admitted to the College in 1945. In 1946, more female students, including Janet Nsibirwa and Anna Bagenda – both teachers – joined the College. Thus the doors to university education were opened to women, never to close again. In 1953, the first women's hall of residence, was completed and named Mary Stuart.

As they mobilised women and prepared them for voting, UCW held sensitisation workshops throughout Uganda on the responsibilities of office holders, how to organise committee membership, fundraising drives, and other related civic engagement activities.

On 23rd March 1961, a nationwide election was held and members were elected to the Internal Self-Government LegCo. This resulted in a victory for the Democratic Party. Its leader, Benedicto Kiwanuka, became the first Prime Minister of Uganda and, therefore, the person who would lead the country into internal self-government (semi-independence). The UCW Sub-committee members took advantage of his new office and led by our legal adviser, Mrs Carol Harlow, we went to see him about a number of issues related to the resolutions of the conference. We requested also that at least one woman be included in the delegation to the Constitutional Conference – the final conference before Independence – that was due to be held in London, in June 1962.

The Prime Minister welcomed our team cheerfully and even served us tea, but he did not grant our request. Perhaps our request came too soon politically for him to convince himself – let alone his cabinet – that a woman's voice was needed in a conference of that importance.

When political parties were preparing their election manifestos and policies in readiness for the general elections that would lead to independence, they reflected a great awareness of the women's movement. This was quite likely because women had the legal right to vote right from the start. The media gave women considerable coverage, although with a hint of ridicule.

The general election that was held on 25th April 1962, was won by the Uganda People's Congress (UPC) and its leader, Apollo Milton Obote, became the Prime Minister. It did not matter much to UCW who held the reins of power. In 1963, soon after the new government was formed, we had a meeting with the Minister for Justice, Grace Ibingira, about the law that would register all marriages. We believed that the move would enhance and establish the status and self-esteem of women and, above all, stabilise society. Fortunately, Ibingira took the issue up with Prime Minister Obote, who readily agreed to create a process that would address the issue. One evening in August 1963 at a YWCA reception, Prime Minister Obote announced that a committee would be appointed to investigate the status of women and recommend reforms to the law that would protect them. He added, "the UCW has been petitioning the government about various aspects of the question. Now their cry has been heard."[6]

The Minister for Justice, Grace Ibingira, later announced the appointment of a commission with William W. Kalema as its chairman. It became known as the Kalema Marriage Commission; formally, it was called the Commission on Marriage, Divorce and the Status of Women. The commission's terms of reference were:

> To consider laws and customs regulating marriage, divorce and the status of women in Uganda, bearing in mind the need to ensure that those laws and customs, while preserving existing traditions and practices as far as possible, should be consistent with justice and morality appropriate to the position of Uganda as an independent nation and to make recommendations.[7]

The other members were Hosea B. Nkojo, Ben Otim Etura, William B. Mwangu and Vincent R. A. C. Crabbe

---

6 Winifred Megaw Brown, *Marriage, Divorce and Inheritance: The Uganda Council of Women's Movement for Legislative Reform* (Cambridge: African Studies Centre, 1988). Page 36.

7 Government of Uganda, *Report of the Commission on Marriage, Divorce and the Status of Women*, Chair: W. W. Kalema (Kampala: Government Printer, 1965), p. 44.

(Ghanaian) as Secretary. We succeeded in getting one woman, Marjorie Kamuhigi Kabuzi, to serve on the commission.

The commission started its work in 1964 and travelled all over the country collecting views. It finally handed its report to the appointing authority on 30th July 1965. Among the recommendations, and perhaps the most significant, was the one that stated, "all marriages, of whatever religion, and whatever nature, should be registered."[8] This was in line with Resolution 13 of the UCW 1960 conference. Although Winifred Brown and Barbara Saben left Uganda and returned to the UK for good in 1965, the task of the UCW sub-committee on the status of women had, to a great extent, been accomplished.

One of Winifred Brown's most significant contributions to the women of Uganda was realised after she settled in Cambridge, England. She documented a lot of the UCW's work, in particular, the mission of the Status of Women sub-committee, in her book, *Marriage, Divorce and Inheritance: The Uganda Council of Women's Movement for Legislative Reform*. It was published in Cambridge in 1988 by the African Studies Centre.[9]

She sent me a copy which, sadly, I lost to a borrower. Later, she sent me 10 reprinted copies (the book was out of print). I gave six copies to the new Department of Women Studies at Makerere University, and two to women organisations. She was very pleased that her book was being shared widely.

The political turmoil in Uganda that started in 1966 and continued thereafter affected follow-ups on the recommendations which had been proposed by women. In 1972,

8   Government of Uganda, p.43.
9   Winifred Megaw Brown, *Marriage, Divorce and Inheritance: The Uganda Council of Women's Movement for Legislative Reform* (Cambridge: African Studies Centre, 1988).

President Idi Amin abolished women organisations apart from a few traditional ones. The first victim was the UCW, with its multinational membership. However, the Mothers' Union, the Catholic Women's Society and the YWCA were left intact. Amin encouraged Muslim women to form their own organisation and in 1978, he decreed the creation of the Uganda National Council of Women, an umbrella women's organisation, under the Ministry of Community Development.

Nevertheless, by this time, the Succession Act had been enacted by parliament in 1967 and a decree of 1972 for the protection of widows was made. This was followed by decree No.16 of 1973 on the registration of all marriages, but it was never implemented. Although successive parliaments debated the Marriage and Divorce Bill many times, up to the time of writing (2021), it had not been passed into law, even after it changed its name to the Domestic Relations Bill.

Pioneers of the Women's Movement: A Tribute

During the formative stages of the Uganda women's movement, three women, Rebecca Mulira, Dorothy Barbara Saben and Eseza Mulira Makumbi were among those who played a distinct role in laying down its foundation. Any discussion about the UCW and women's progress in Uganda would be incomplete without the mention of these distinguished women. They were among the women who used their privileged backgrounds, education and experiences to promote women's education, leadership skills and social justice. They had great leadership qualities and I owe a lot to them. It was mainly through working with them that I was mentored into leadership and in developing a commitment to women's concerns. It is in this light that I want to pay special tribute to them.

REBECCA MULIRA and I had a lot in common and our fathers were close friends, just as we were. She was a tall, impressive and very confident woman who had a God-given gift for farsightedness and goodwill. She was motivated to do everything in her power to work towards her passion and creed – the advancement of women's social and political status. She was a great mentor and we had great fun together.

Born into a large family of the prominent Chief, Hamu Mukasa, the *saza* chief of Kyagwe County, and his wife Sala, Rebecca was educated at Gayaza High School – like her mother before her. She got married to Eridadi Mulira, a teacher who was a staunch Christian and they had two daughters and five sons. Her mother was one of the early members of the Mothers' Union in Uganda, in 1914.

Rebecca was a founder member of the UCW in 1946 and she served as the organisation's national president in 1962. She was also a founder member of the Young Wives Group (a junior Mothers' Union) and was the group's first president. In 1953, she was president of the Forward Society – a young women's group that was established to enhance the members' formal education. She was in Britain in 1951 when the general election that returned the Prime Minister, Sir Winston Churchill, was held. She noted how active the British women were and she resolved to be more politically engaged when she returned to Uganda. Ten years later, in 1961, she vied for a seat in the Buganda *Lukiiko*. In the FOWODE monograph, *A Rising Tide*, Rebecca notes:

> "I thought I was going to be successful but I was not. This was because of men. They went around at night kneeling before people telling them that the Kabaka did not want women in the *Lukiiko* as yet. I went straight to the Kabaka's palace after the

election… and told him exactly what happened. He said he had nothing to do with it. So he appointed me a member of Mengo Municipal Council and at the same time a member of Kampala City Council. Other women too did not go through in the election. I told them we were going to continue fighting these men".[10]

When Rebecca returned from a YWCA study programme, she stated, "We want to include everyone regardless of the word 'Christian' because we want to work for all the women of Uganda."[11] Muslim women were reluctant to join the YWCA, so Rebecca and her colleagues appealed for support from Prince Badru Kakungulu, the leader of the Muslims in Buganda. The Prince responded, "I went to King's College Budo because Muslims during those years had no schools. Had I not gone to Budo, I would not have been as useful to the Muslim community as I am now. I will see to it that all Muslim women join the YWCA."[12] And join they did, including the Prince's wife.

Through the years, Rebecca served on the board of the Mulago Hospital and many school, college boards, and church committees in Uganda. In 1964, Mrs Golda Meir, who was then the Foreign Minister of Israel, invited her to a conference on the role of women in the struggle for peace and development. In 1971, as the president of the Family Planning Association of Uganda, she attended a meeting in New Delhi, India, where she met the Prime Minister, Mrs Indira Gandhi. In 1995 she joined the Uganda delegation to the Women's Decade Conference in Beijing, China.

---

10 Winnie Byanyima and Richard Mugisha, *"A Rising Tide: Ugandan Women's Struggle for a Public Voice 1940-2004"*, Forum for Women in Democracy (FOWODE), Kampala, 2005.

11 Byanyima and Mugisha, "A Rising Tide".

12 Ibid.

Through the YWCA and UCW, she visited women's groups all over Uganda, from Teso to Gulu, Mbarara, Mbale and Karamoja – sharing what she had garnered from her work and travels. Rebecca wished passionately for all women to grow and progress with her. In 2006, the YWCA headquarters in Kampala named one of its facilities, 'Rebecca Mulira Resource Centre', in honour of her, as a founder and trustee.

Rebecca passed away on 9th November 2001, aged 81.

DOROTHY BARBARA SABEN, C.B.E. was a strong pillar in the emancipation of Ugandan women. Barbara and her husband Timothy "Timmie", a businessman, were British. Though I never got to know when they arrived in Uganda, records indicate that during the early 1940s, she was one of the pioneers of the Uganda Women's League which transformed into the UCW. Together with Alice Boase, they were the first two women to be nominated by the colonial government to the LegCo in the 1950s.

Barbara's outstanding involvements include lobbying the LegCo to have a YWCA girls' hostel built to promote girls' education and to provide affordable accommodation for those working in town. She also worked tirelessly to improve the welfare and accommodation of women prisoners, notably, by installing running water in prisons. She led fellow LegCo women members in persuading the government to allow women to vote in the 1961 and 1962 general elections.

Barbara was the first, and up to the time of writing this book, the only female Mayor of Kampala, a role she executed superbly. She was always elegantly dressed, cheerful, encouraging, courageous, sociable and a devoted mother to her two sons. She died on 30th September 2014, at the age of 102 years.

Eseza Mulira Makumbi was a tower of strength to the
Uganda women's movement. She was a servant leader who
used every opportunity to promote social justice for all. Born
into a prominent family in Buganda in 1918, she was educated
at the Gayaza High School. In 1935, she trained as a teacher
and taught English at the Buloba Teacher Training College
and King's College Budo. In 1943, she got married to Thomas
Makumbi, a renowned teacher and a graduate of Cambridge
University. They had eight children.

Eseza was also an actress. In 1946, she starred in a British
film, *Men of Two Worlds*. The film was about an educated,
successful, African musician in Britain who decides to return
to his village to help educate his people about modern living
and better health practices. A review of the film in *The Spectator*
magazine, in July 1946, commented on "the beautiful voice as
well as the beautiful looks of Eseza Makumbi, who plays the
musician's sister."

Driven by her great concern for justice for women and
their dignity, she was at the forefront of the UCW resolution
in 1958 that sought to reform marriage laws. In the 1950s,
under the pen-name 'Maliza', she was one of four women
(two British and one Asian) who wrote a regular column for
the *Uganda Argus*. 'Maliza' is the local pronounciation of the
Biblical name Martha and is taken from the Biblical story
where Martha did the work behind the scenes while her sister
Mary entertained Jesus[13]. The 'Maliza' column successfully
drew a clear distinction between significant matters and
mundane issues that have little or no impact on women's lives.

---

13 In Luke 10:38-42 when Jesus and His disciples visited two sisters at their home, Mary "sat at the
Lord's feet listening to what he said. But Martha was distracted by all the preparations that had
to be made. She came to him and asked, "Lord, don't you care that my sister has left me to do
the work by myself? Tell her to help me!" "Martha, Martha," the Lord answered, "you are worried
and upset about many things, but few things are needed—or indeed only one. Mary has chosen
what is better, and it will not be taken away from her." (NIV).

In the 1950s, the colonial Governor of Uganda appointed Eseza to the LegCo and in 1962, to the East African Common Services Organisation Parliament. It was, therefore, appropriate that during the celebrations that marked Uganda's Golden Jubilee Independence in October 2012, she was honoured with a Women Achievers' Award for her outstanding work by the Uganda Women's Parliamentary Association and Uganda Women's Network (UWONET) which embraces all voluntary women organisations. Eseza passed away on 21st September 2014, aged 96.

Chapter 9

The Sixties – A Defining Decade

The 1960s were eventful, not just for me, but also for Uganda. The period started with the convening of the first women's conference in March 1960 that helped me fully realise the important role women's emancipation played in a country's development. In August, our fourth child, Apolo Katerega, was born, and the following year, a series of political events took place in quick succession culminating in the independence of Uganda in October 1962. Sadly, the decade also closed with the shocking death of Kabaka Edward Frederick Mutesa II, in London, in November 1969.

Birth of Apolo Serwano Katerega

On 23rd August 1960, we welcomed Apolo Katerega, our fourth child, who was born at Mengo Hospital. At the time, all his siblings were enrolled in school. Betty, our eldest and only girl, had wished for a baby sister and her cousin, Joy, shared in her short-lived disappointment. They got over it and loved him dearly. Apolo was born when my career as a social worker was in its early stages, and I was torn when I had to leave him at only four months to attend the conference in Ghana.

Uganda's Independence Day, 1962

On 9th October 1962, Uganda celebrated the attainment of her independence. It was the greatest historical event in the country. Because of its history and role in the Buganda Agreement of 1900 with Britain, the Buganda Kingdom was offered a special independence day, the 8th of October, a day before the National Independence Day.

I found myself personally involved in some national duties, including appointment to the Buganda Kingdom's independence organising committee. The other members were Asanasio Masembe, the Head of Palace Operations (*Mukulu w'oLubiri*), Eriver Kigundu, Kabaka's Secretary, Yunia Kamanyi, the President of The Mothers Union, and Mr Musisi, a top official at the palace.

Since Uganda had been a British Protectorate, Her Majesty Queen Elizabeth II was represented at the celebrations by the Royal Highnesses, the Duke and Duchess of Kent – Prince Edward and his wife Katherine – who were also scheduled to preside over the Buganda independence ceremony at the Buganda *Lukiiko* (Parliament). The Duke and Duchess visited several places separately after the *Lukiiko* ceremony and I was in the Duchess' entourage. She viewed a display of handicrafts at the *Lubiri* and was given beautiful handmade traditional gifts.

Later that day, I was with her when she unveiled a plaque to officially open the new Mulago Hospital, an independence gift from the British Government. A plaque with her name, commemorating the event, is on the hospital's fourth floor.

The constitution that was promulgated that year had a provision for twenty-one specially elected Members of Parliament from Buganda. The members joined parliament as *Kabaka Yekka* (KY), meaning, King Only. In the general election countrywide, outside Buganda, the UPC had a narrow majority over the Democratic Party. The UPC-KY alliance formed the first government's side in parliament after independence. William Kalema was among the twenty-one specially elected members. Apollo Milton Obote, the leader of the UPC, became the Prime Minister. A year later, the Kabaka, Edward Fredrick Mutesa II, became the President of Uganda, replacing the Queen of England as the Head of State.

UNESCO's 12th General Conference

As the new government settled in, an invitation from UNESCO headquarters in Paris to the Ministry of Education requested that the government send a delegation to its twelfth World Conference that was to be held in November 1962, in Paris. The theme was 'Science and Technology'. Rebecca Mulira and I were pleasantly surprised by our inclusion in the delegation that also comprised the Minister of Education, Dr Joshua Luyimbazi Zake and one top officer from his ministry. When we arrived in Paris, we only had a faint idea about the theme. I still recall how several delegates spoke intensely – mostly in French and other international languages – about the important role science and technology would play in the future. Although there were translators present, it did not make much sense to either of us then, and outside the conference we joked about the science and technology theme, believing that the concepts being deliberated were too advanced for our young nation.

However, we gained a lot from the exposure and learnt what UNESCO was all about. The experience also gave us the confidence to continue working for women's emancipation and participation in politics. I have since visited historic heritage sites that have been adopted by UNESCO in different countries, including the Kasubi Tombs – the burial site of Buganda's kings, and the Masada, an ancient fortress in Israel.

Rebecca and I decided to wear our Kiganda *busuti* for the duration of the conference and our outfits drew great attention at the conference and on the streets. Many people stopped to greet us and ask about our dress and country. I was impressed by the beauty of Paris, especially the iconic Eiffel Tower and the Champs-Elysées.

Birth of Veronica Sara Mirembe Nakibule

Even during the early independence years, African government employees did not get maternity leave. Our daughter, Naki, as she is popularly known at home, was born on 5th October 1964, under the prevailing unfavourable civil service rules, as was our son, Apolo Katerega. Looking back, I am astonished at how I managed it all fairly smoothly as a mother and housewife with a government job – in charge of the main Probation and Welfare Office, in Kampala.

Like her older siblings, all her names were special to us. 'Veronica' was my mother's name, 'Sara' was my dear late sister, and 'Mirembe' (peace) was given because she was born on Peace Day—a historical day that marks the armistice in the 1880s during the inter-religious wars in Buganda. In the 1960s, 5th October was still celebrated annually as a Peace Day. Nakibule was William's eldest sister and Naki's paternal aunt. Naki later became her aunt's cultural heir.

Princess Margaret's Visit

In March 1965, I had yet another royal to chaperone when I joined the entourage of Her Royal Highness, Princess Margaret, the Countess of Snowdon, who was on a ten-day state visit to Uganda with her husband, Lord Snowdon.

Princess Margaret was Queen Elizabeth II's younger sister; they were the only children of King George VI. I cannot recall the specific purpose of their visit, except that they were the guests of the new Ugandan government and the Kabaka of Buganda. The entourage included men and women from Ugandan and British governments. Princess Margaret was also accompanied by her own special entourage. The royal couple visited Tororo Girls' School in the East, the Murchison Falls, and the Queen Elizabeth National Parks in western Uganda. They received a joyous welcome wherever they went, especially from women groups.

Princess Margaret charmed many and people commented on her beauty. I remember Nalinya (Princess) Irene Ndagire, who was herself very beautiful, commenting in Luganda, "*Aaah, buno obulungi tebuliiko mpaka!*" (literally, "Surely, there is no debate about her great beauty").

British Council Study Visit to Britain

Later, in October 1965, the British Council invited a group of Ugandan women, wives of top government officials, to Britain. They were Solome Sentongo, wife of Jack Sentongo, the Secretary to the Treasury; Flora Bigirwenkya, wife of Z. K. Bigirwenkya, a Permanent Secretary in the Ministry of Foreign Affairs; Freda Kikira whose husband was a District Commissioner in the eastern region; and I, the wife of the Minister for Works, Housing and Communications. It seems that the visit's objective was to give Ugandan women in positions of influence exposure to the British social, economic and cultural way of life.

We left Uganda on a British Overseas Airways Corporation flight to London and we were put up at the St Ermin's Hotel in Westminster. On the month long tour, we visited prominent places like Buckingham Palace, Westminster Abbey, Trafalgar Square, St Paul's Cathedral and the Houses of Parliament. Also very impressive was the tour of the London headquarters of the retail chain, Marks and Spencer. Our guide recounted its interesting history that started when two friends, Michael Marks and Thomas Spencer, made and sold buttons and thread in 1884 and eventually, from humble beginnings, created one of the biggest retail stores in the world.

We were informed that Mrs Khrushchev, the wife of the Soviet Union leader, would travel to London every summer to buy a year's stock of stockings in the store. Many shoppers also travelled from as far as Australia and America to buy Marks and Spencer goods, which were considered quality and reasonably priced. In Uganda, there was a shop on Kampala Road called Deacons which sold Marks and Spencer clothing with the St Michael's label.

On our last two days, Ian Smith, the leader of the British colonialists in Southern Rhodesia (now Zimbabwe), was in the UK as a guest of the British Government and he stayed at St Ermin's. I remember the press jostling to take his photograph as he got in and out of his car. The newspapers stated that Smith was head of a delegation of British colonialists from Southern Rhodesia who were in Britain for crucial discussions about the country's self-rule. Shortly thereafter, he declared Rhodesia's unilateral independence, and the result was many years' of war with African freedom fighters.

The 1966 Mengo crisis

Unresolved issues regarding the power and status of the Buganda Kingdom and its king within the nation of Uganda came up after independence. Matters came to a head on 22nd February 1966, when Prime Minister Obote arrested five of his cabinet ministers in the middle of a cabinet meeting, abrogated the constitution and dismissed the President (the Kabaka of Buganda, Sir Edward Mutesa II). On 24th May, there was an attack on his *Lubiri* at Mengo by sections of the Uganda army, led by Colonel Idi Amin. This caused an unprecedented constitutional crisis which had far-reaching repercussions that set off decades of political turmoil in our country. The extent of the violence frightened everyone. At the time, I was admitted in the Mulago Hospital, on my doctor's advice, after I experienced a series of health problems. The hospital, on a hill overlooking Kampala, also faces Mengo Hill. Amidst a heavy downpour, we heard loud explosions. We were shaken and anxious, with no idea of what was going on.

The immediate outcome of this violent attack was the Kabaka's flight to and exile in Britain. His miraculous escape from the siege sparked speculation that he had applied the military skills learnt as a Colonel in the Queen's Grenadier Guards. Many innocent people were killed in the palace that day including the *Mukulu w'Olubiri* (Head of Palace Operations), Asanansio Masembe. Sebsequently kingdoms of Buganda, Bunyoro, Ankole and Tooro were abolished in September 1967 by Prime Minister Obote.

While the Kabaka managed to escape to safety and into exile, Lady Damali and her sister Sarah, both wives of the Kabaka, were locked up at the Luzira Prison. In his book, *Desecration of my Kingdom*, Kabaka Mutesa observed: "I heard that my wife and her sister Sarah were in prison, but did not know whether to believe it. I also heard that they were treated appallingly."[14]

Yes, they were treated appallingly. The two sisters and royal wives were victims of circumstances. I was allowed,

---

14 Mutesa II (King of Buganda), *Desecration of My Kingdom* (London, Constable, 1967), p. 18.

through a prison wardress, to send them some basic toiletries like toothpaste, soap, and towels.

Commonwealth Parliamentary Association

During those years, I was involved, to some extent, in my husband's work. I travelled with him outside the country and those journeys and experiences became part of my story. One of those experiences was related to the Commonwealth Parliamentary Association (CPA), a body that works to promote parliamentary democracy in Commonwealth countries by developing and supporting parliamentarians and their staff. The association held regular meetings that were hosted alternately by member states.

When the CPA annual conference was held in New Zealand in 1965, William was elected Vice-Chairman for 1965/66. One year later, he became its chairman and in 1967, Uganda hosted the 13th CPA Conference.

In May 1967, William, who was Minister for Works, attended meetings in New York and Washington DC and I accompanied him. From what I remember, the purpose of the trip was to acquire machinery for building roads. My indelible memory of New York was the visit to the Empire State Building. It had been completed in 1931 and, at the time, with 102 floors, it was the tallest building in the world. When we visited the great landmark, we were whisked in a lift to the top from where we viewed the whole of New York. It was a great experience. It was fashionable for anyone visiting the Empire State Building to have a photo taken and we, too, posed for one. I treasure the memory.

The second leg of the trip took us to Malta for three days. While there, William, as CPA Chairman, attended a meeting to plan for the CPA conference scheduled to be held in Kampala. My vivid memory of Malta was that it was almost a desert country – the little that I saw.

However, I also remember seeing dark green patches in the distance. We were informed that those were agricultural areas in oases where Malta's main food crops – potatoes, vegetables and fruits – were grown for local consumption and export. The latter activity we learnt, earned Malta substantial foreign exchange. I was amazed at what a small country with focussed targets can do with its resources.

In October, William chaired the CPA Conference in Uganda's parliament building. The conference was attended by representatives of all CPA member countries. A variety of African, Caribbean, Asian and Western traditional attires were showcased. I was in a photo on the front row next to the Chairman, dressed in my Kiganda *busuti*. Also in the photo were President Apollo Milton Obote, the Chief Justice, Udo Udoma and the Speaker of the Uganda parliament, Narendra Patel.

Uganda Women's Hockey Association

In 1967, a year after I retired from public service, Mr Anywar, a retired police officer, and the President of the Uganda Men's Hockey Association (UMHA), approached me. He asked if I would accept to be the President of the Uganda Women's Hockey Association (UWHA) and offer the team support. I had played a bit of hockey at King's College Budo, where the sport was mostly a boy's game. Since I had rested for a year, I readily accepted his request.

The main teams in the association were mostly from secondary schools, Makerere College School and St Mary's Namagunga as well as some young female secretaries – mostly

Asians who were working in Kampala. I was encouraged when I found out that the young women had a passion for hockey. For instance, the headmistress of Namagunga, Sister Anselm, who instilled character and confidence in the students of her time, allowed the girls, in their short hockey skirts, to travel the twenty-two miles by public transport to play in Kampala at Lugogo Sports Grounds and return to school in the evening after their game. Many of these girls, who brought pride to their schools, later became outstanding women in society in their chosen professions.

Mrs Hannah Lule, the wife of Professor Yusuf Kironde Lule, the then Principal of Makerere College, agreed to be the Vice President of the UWHA. During her time at King's College Budo, Hannah was a great sportswoman. She would outrun everyone.

By August 1968, we had a good team and raised enough money to send it to the Afro-Asian tournament in New Delhi. Half of the team consisted of Asian girls – and the other half, black Ugandans. The team was led by two great supporters of the UWHA, Mr Sandhu, a member of the UMHA and Mrs Miriam Sozi, the wife of Michael Sozi, the headmaster of Makerere College School. The team was second in the tournament and they brought home a silver trophy. When they returned, the team captain, Harjeet Sandhu and her deputy, Freda Lule (Hannah Lule's daughter), handed the trophy to the Minister for Culture and Community Development, Hon. C.B. Katiiti. It was then handed over to the National Council of Sports.

Years later, when writing this book, I met a woman after a burial ceremony and she greeted me cheerfully so I asked who she was. "I am Josephine Mukasa, a former Namagunga student and member of the Women Hockey Association," she replied. "Your team at UWHA took us to New Delhi and we brought back a trophy after securing second place." I then learnt that she had gone on to work at Makerere University after her studies and when we met, she was working at Nkumba University.

Setting up a Family Home in Kiboga

My husband's big vision and ambition for his home area was to see it develop. Hence, in 1967, he decided to establish a permanent family home in Kiboga. He particularly wanted a home with access to electricity and telephone services, which were not available on the family land near his father's home, five miles from Kiboga Town. Thus it became necessary to buy land in Kiboga Town. William also had a political agenda. He confided, "I wish to represent my people more effectively after the next general elections."

Construction began in earnest and the house was completed within eight months, in August 1968. We built an underground water tank and electricity and telephone services were also connected. It was our dream home and since it had all the necessary facilities, it was very comfortable. We loved hosting our many friends and extended families in it. By then, we had five children. Unfortunately for William, this bliss only lasted about two years.

During the chaos that accompanied Idi Amin's *coup d'état* in January 1971, our home suffered a major blow; it was looted and every moveable thing – windows, doors, furniture, utensils and bedding were taken. We had also put up a commercial building in Kiboga town and it, too was looted. Many years later, I still remembered how much this blow affected my husband's spirit. He had invested a lot of resources and so much sentiment into everything and it was not surprising that he became dejected. All the same, he did not give up on life altogether.

* * *

As the 1960s decade drew to a close, our family was saddened by the untimely death of my dear brother, Sira Bugembe, at Mulago Hospital on 30th October 1968, aged forty-four after he suffered a brain haemorrhage.

Death of Kabaka Mutesa II

The sixties closed with the great shock and sadness that engulfed the country at the death of Kabaka Edward Frederick Mutesa II on 21st November 1969, in London – two days after his birthday. He was just forty-five years old. In his book, *Three Worlds: One Word – Account of a Mission*, the former Archbishop of Uganda, the Rt Reverend Leslie Brown, wrote:

> "On the night of 19 November 1969, his birthday, I telephoned him as I generally did on that day, and spoke to him briefly in Luganda, giving him my birthday wishes. On 22 November, he was found dead. The funeral service was in the Guards' Chapel, as he had been a Grenadier officer. At Kensal Green Cemetery a funeral service was held and the body committed to a vault, to await removal to Uganda. I took this service in Luganda, assisted by the Dean of Namirembe and the Roman Catholic Bishop of Masaka, who had flown to England to be there. The Kabaka's wife, Damali, was also present. It was a bizarre and sad end to a man who had great gifts and could be the most attractive and agreeable friend[15].

15 Leslie Brown, *Three Worlds: One Word - Account of a Mission* (London: Collins, 1981), p231

Encounter with Corrie ten Boom

In the late 1960s, somebody whose name I cannot recall, introduced me to Mr and Mrs Ernest Lohrer who lived in Switzerland. They were a Christian couple and although we never met, we corresponded, exchanging mail and Christmas greetings for some years, and they played a part in my spiritual growth.

In 1970, the Lohrers told me about one Cornelia Arnolda Johanna, aka "Corrie" ten Boom. They informed me that the Dutchwoman, a survivor of a Nazi concentration camp in World War II, was scheduled to visit Uganda and speak at the Lweza Conference Centre, on the invitation of Christians who were working at the Mengo Hospital. I attended her one-day conference and although she spoke English with a Dutch accent, we all understood her astonishing message of salvation. Her testimony about the reality of God's love, in the worst situations one can imagine, was very powerful. It shook many people.

Corrie ten Boom was born on 15th April 1892, in Amsterdam, Netherlands, the youngest in her family. She told of how they suffered during World War II. Her father, Casper ten Boom, rescued and hid Jews before he and his family were betrayed and arrested. He died in prison and Corrie and her sister Betsie were transported to the Ravensbruck Concentration Camp, where Betsie also died. Corrie was released from Ravensbruck through a clerical error; the only survivor in her entire family.

Looking back, I believe that God was preparing me for the political conflict that would engulf my own country in a year's time, and the loss of my beloved husband in 1972, in a cruel manner, under mysterious circumstances. When Corrie returned home to California, I wrote to her and she responded. In a signed letter dated 14th September 1972, she sent me precious Bible texts to comfort me, including 1 Peter 5:7 (NIV) which states: "Cast all your anxiety on Him, because He cares for you."

My name was added to her mailing list and I started receiving pamphlets and books from her. These included, *The Hiding Place,* a memoir, *Bereavement* and *In My Father's House.* I still have many of her books which I read often and share with other people. I continued to correspond with Corrie ten Boom's secretariat and that is how I learnt that she had died on 16th April, 1983. Reading Corrie's books and testimonies about suffering made me realise that knowing God deeply privileges us to understand that our suffering is not outside His care, love, or faithfulness. These are constant and He still fulfills His purposes in our lives even through our suffering. The Bible states, for example, "And we know that in all things God works for the good of those who love Him" (Romans 8:28-30, NIV)

I met Corrie ten Boom only once, about 50 years ago, and I still marvel at God's plan that brought this woman evangelist into my life at that particular time.

Chapter 10

Death of My Husband

When Major-General Idi Amin Dada, the Army Commander, overthrew the government of President Milton Obote, he set off a tragic turn of events in the country. A violent change of government usually shakes everyone, including those in government, but more so, those in the cabinet. The coup, therefore, affected my family directly even as it changed the direction of the entire nation.

The January 1971 Coup

The Amin-led military *coup d'état* was executed on 25th January 1971, as President Apollo Milton Obote was on a flight on his way back from a Commonwealth Heads of Government Meeting (CHOGM) in Singapore. William was the Minister for Commerce and Industry at the time, and was among those in President Obote's entourage. Also in the entourage were Sam Odaka, the Minister for Foreign Affairs; Henry Kyemba, the Principal Private Secretary to the President, and Paul Etyang who was then Uganda's High Commissioner to the United Kingdom.

During the Bombay-Nairobi leg of the trip, the pilot received a call warning that there was fighting raging in

Uganda. He communicated the message to President Obote and the rest of the delegation. After a short while, the pilot announced that because the Entebbe Airport was under the control of hostile sections of the army, they were going to land in Nairobi, Kenya. President Obote and his entourage spent a few hours in Kenya, before flying to Dar es Salaam where President Nyerere offered them asylum.

By virtue of their positions, the cabinet ministers were likely to be victims of the coup alongside President Obote. So, while the civil servants in the delegation returned to Uganda almost immediately, my husband returned a few weeks later. Sam Odaka remained in exile until after the fall of Idi Amin, in 1979.

Besides the military takeover being unprecedented, the coup was scary. Explosions from the fighting could be heard clearly all over the city. I was at home on 16 Philip Road, in Kololo, with our youngest four – Peter Martin, Katerega, Nakibule, and Gladys Rhoda Nalubowa Nantale, who was born on 8th January 1970. We lived in a government house so first thing in the morning, we moved out. Fortunately, my brother, Kiwana, had a large family house with a self-contained basement apartment nearby. The apartment served as the Kalema home until June 1971. With Betty and William Jnr away at University, we managed well in the limited but comfortable and secure accommodation as I waited for William's return.

The entire presidential entourage was confined in one place in Dar es Salaam. William knew that he was in a precarious and dangerous situation and communicating was a problem. However, he later told me, despite the potential danger to himself, he decided he had to find a way and means of returning home.

Eventually, his good friend in Uganda, James Mulwana, managed to arrange for his return. He was aided by Mr Wolfe, a close German business associate who owned a light aircraft. He offered it and William was smuggled from Dar-es-Salaam via Nairobi's Wilson Airport to Entebbe. I was informed about the plan at the last minute. Immediately, I plucked up courage and went to see Idi Amin at his 'Command Post' in Kololo. "My husband wishes to return to Uganda," I said to Amin. "I request that he be allowed a secure arrival and stay in the country." President Amin agreed to my request without hesitation.

On 12th February 1971, William returned and Amin directed one of his ministers, Abu Mayanja, the Minister for Education, to go and officially meet him at Entebbe Airport. This gesture provided William with safe cover and a chance to meet Mayanja, a long-time friend. William and Abu had a long history, that went back to the time when William was a teacher and Abu a student at King's College Budo. They were then both political activists in Britain and Uganda through the 1950s and 1960s. I doubt that Amin knew about their relationship. At the time of the coup, Abu Mayanja was a political prisoner. He was appointed Minister for Education in Idi Amin's government. When William saw me at the airport with Abu Mayanja on arrival, he felt at ease and the many probing questions from journalists did not bother him.

On reaching Kampala, the police asked him to hand over his passport and he was also ordered to always seek permission if he wished to travel outside the city. Despite the many movements restrictions, he was relieved and happy to return home to his family, because, as he said, it was all he had left in life. He confessed that when he was in Dar-es-Salaam, he worried because he thought that his family and relatives would be victimised by the authorities.

Nakasero Road Home

To ensure that we had security, William did not want us to move back to our suburban home in Muyenga so he started looking for a house to buy in the city centre. He found one on Nakasero Road, in central Kampala and we moved in on 1st June, 1971. I remember that, amidst the chaos of moving and luggage and other property strewn all over the place, he lay on our unmade bed and said with a great sigh of relief, "Now, even if I were to die, I would know where I have left my family."

The house was very old; its title deed was registered in 1925, but it was very solid and roomy. Most importantly, it was in a central location and therefore a great asset. However, we had to carry out some improvements, like fixing built-in bedroom wardrobes and kitchen cupboards. We settled down and, although we had mixed feelings – both relief and apprehension – at least we were together once again, in our home.

Ten years earlier, William had bought a life insurance policy in my name with Crusader Insurance Co. Ltd. The policy matured around the time that we moved and that is the money that we used to improve our new home. We had a large compound where the children enjoyed playing. It even had a tennis court. William adjusted easily to the new life and he started considering investment opportunities as he paid off the loan he had taken from the Housing Finance Company to buy the home.

At the time, he said he had three wishes to fulfil regarding his family. One, was the removal of six-year-old Nakibule's tonsils because she suffered from frequent infections. This was done in November 1971. When he visited her in the hospital, he took her flowers and Naki has always cherished the memory of her father taking her flowers. Second, he wanted us to celebrate Betty's 21st birthday when she came home for the holidays. Although we did not have much money to spare, she had a successful party at home with her friends and cousins and we had to bear with the noise and jubilation late into the night. His third wish was to visit his mother in Kikoloto village in Kiboga Sub-county before the end of the year. It was going to be their first meeting since his return from Dar es Salaam.

Visit to Kiboga

The order that William had to request permission whenever he wished to travel outside Kampala was still in place, and it was always granted. Just before Christmas, we travelled with our children – except the youngest, baby Nalubowa and William Jnr.

On arrival, our first stop was at our home that was looted during the coup. When William heard about the looting when he was in Dar es Salaam, he was very distressed. He and the children saw, for the first time, the ruins of the home to which we had attached so much sentiment. I had already visited the house with my sister, Eseza Kironde and my youngest son, Katerega, but not before asking for a security escort from President Amin.

Everything was gone, except the walls and the tiles on the roof. It was heartbreaking to see the wanton destruction of the things that the looters did not manage to carry or use including the electric cooker and bathtub. We photographed the back of the house. William was numb. He just said, "It is hard to see all my efforts and money lost in such a way." He did not mention anything to suggest that he planned to restore our 'dream home.'

When we finally reached his mother's home, it was a joy to see mother and son embrace. It was the realisation of hope that had been lost before William's return home ten months earlier. It was a very emotional occasion for all of us. Little did we realise that it was a divinely planned visit; that the moment would never be experienced again in our family's life. We returned to Kampala that evening. It was a long, sad return journey of about 200 miles. The last picture we took with William's mother holds precious memories.

At Christmas, we joined our extended family and friends for a picnic lunch at Lutembe Beach. We would later regard this occasion as another divine moment when our larger family and friends interacted with William for the last time. The friends included Paul and Freda Marchant from Winchester, England, old friends of my sister Janet Mdoe and her husband, who had eventually become friends of the entire Nsibirwa family. A photograph of William and Paul taken on that day, also brings back great memories.

William's Kidnapping and Disappearance

For some time after his return, William was very apprehensive about his safety. Having accompanied President Obote to the Commonwealth Summit, and also having been a cabinet minister in the ousted government, he feared for his life. Alas, his fears were not unfounded. At about 6.30 pm, on 20th January 1972, almost a year after the coup, William was kidnapped. We believe that he was killed on that very day.

It is difficult for me to relate the events around William's kidnapping. First of all, the memory is extremely painful, and time has not really healed much of the pain because one's spouse becomes part of one's life and, therefore, part of their treasured life-story. As our family contemplated the shocking matter, and as the days and weeks passed, I tried to piece together some explanation for the regime's actions that led to my husband's 'disappearance'.

While I shall never know exactly what single force or combination of forces led to William's death, I suspect that false information about his Uganda Commercial Bank (UCB) account could have sparked the events that took his life. We found out about this on the morning of 20th January, when the UCB Managing Director, Chris Kabenge, who was a friend, came to our house. He said he had a secret to tell William. William ushered him into our bedroom and asked me to leave the two of them alone. Chris left soon afterwards. In the bedroom, I found William sitting on the bed with his head bowed, deep in thought. I asked him what Kabenge had told him.

"Yesterday," he said, "certain men from the State Research Bureau (SRB) went to UCB and asked for the Impala House accounts." William was one of the partners who owned Impala Properties (now Impala House), a building in the city. Others were Jack Sentongo, Shafiq Arain, and Gurdial Singh. Shortly before William was kidnapped, the partners sold the property and divided the proceeds among the shareholders. SRB had received information that money from that account had been sent to Milton Obote by William Kalema. The men had gone to UCB to look for evidence.

The SRB had been created in February 1971, by presidential decree. Initially, it was meant to be a military intelligence and counter-intelligence service but it rapidly transformed into a multipurpose security unit as Idi Amin decreed sweeping powers for his non-uniformed officers. The agency started targeting civilians and gradually, its operations spread to all corners of the country, terrorising people with extreme impunity. Before long, SRB became known for torture, extortion and extrajudicial executions; and earned its reputation as the most dreaded security agency in Uganda. Its officers could easily be identified by their flamboyant dress and the dark glasses they wore.

When they failed to find the evidence that they were looking for, they threw papers on the floor, grumbling and annoyed. "We cannot see anything here as they told us," they complained as they left.

It is possible that a political enemy of William spread the lie. It was strange that Idi Amin, who had welcomed his return from exile following the coup just a year earlier, would choose to believe the lie, despite evidence seen by his own intelligence officers that no money had been transferred to Obote. As I look back later after extended experience with tyrannical governance, I know that tyrants are always very insecure about anything they imagine could threaten their power, and in their paranoia, they often react brutally. William was one of Amin's imaginary enemies.

Later that day, after William went into town, I too left and took our daughter Nakibule and her cousins Miriam and Hansa Wambuzi swimming at the Makerere University swimming pool. I also took two-year-old Nalubowa along for the outing. We returned home at around six o'clock in the evening and I dropped off our girls before taking my two young nieces to their home nearby. I spoke briefly to William through the window as he was also preparing to take Mary Namazzi, a relative, back to her home in Kansanga, about five miles away. I expected that we would both be home by eight o'clock to listen to the news and have dinner together as usual. However, that glance through the bedroom window was the last time that our eyes met and the short conversation, our last.

When William left the house with Mary, two vehicles outside our gate, that had men wearing dark glasses in them, followed him at high speed and one overtook him. About half a mile from Mary's house, at the bend where Kabalagala Police Station now stands, they intercepted him. Onlookers reported that William was told to leave his car and get into the intercepting car. One of the men entered William's car, a BMW (registration number UUM 579) and they all took off.

Our good friend, James Mulwana, happened to be driving home in the opposite direction at the time. Seeing William in the strange car, he waved at him, but William did not respond. James later realised that William had appeared fearful. At about eight o'clock, James called wishing to speak to William. When I told him that he was not yet home, James insisted that I ask him to call him as soon as he returned. After thirty minutes, James called again. When I told him William was not back yet, he drove to our house. By then, I was really afraid. I called family and friends asking if they had seen him. Nobody had, except James who caught a glimpse of him as he was being driven away. I believe that God wanted to leave a trail of William's disappearance so he let James notice him. Some women standing near the spot where William was abducted only realised later, with shock, what they had witnessed. "Was

Kalema being kidnapped as we watched?" they asked.

At midnight, accompanied by my brother-in-law, Erisa Kironde, I went to the Central Police Station to report that my husband had not returned home. I spent the rest of that night at the home of Justice Wambuzi and his wife, my sister Gladys. Expecting a call at any moment, I did not sleep. Four of our children were home, Peter Martin (17), Katerega (11), Nakibule (7) and Nalubowa (2). Peter and Kateregga were very disturbed when their father did return that night.

When I returned home at the break of day, Peter was weeping. He told me that the previous evening, as he left home on his way to visit friends at Makerere just before his father left, he had seen two vehicles parked on the road outside our gate. He recalled that one was a blue Peugeot estate car and that there were men wearing dark glasses seated in the cars. "When Taata went through the gate soon after, these two cars followed him at high speed," he said. Peter said he did not pay much attention to them. He later said that he had almost asked his father if he could accompany him. In hindsight, we realised that his hesitation was an intervention and blessing from God. Anyone travelling in the same car with William that evening would have been sacrificed to eliminate any evidence. Mary, our relative, was never seen again.

We informed the children, Betty and William who were at university, and my husband's mother and his family in faraway Kiboga, about his abduction. Erisa Kironde informed our son at Cambridge through Godfrey Kavuma, a family friend. Betty managed to come home for a few days before going back to University of Nairobi to continue her studies. At the time, Betty was twenty-one and William Jr was twenty. It was later reported that William's car had crossed Uganda's western border, into Congo.

* * *

We clung to the hope that William was in some detention centre or military barrack since there was no trace of him or his body. The SRB headquarters was on Nakasero Hill near the Presidential Lodge and, ironically, not far from our home. Hope was the only straw that we could cling on. However, the headquarters was a total no-go area.

While we were still hoping that William would 're-appear,' we received a scare through a government announcement on Radio Uganda. "People reporting their relatives to the police as 'disappeared' must be absolutely clear about their report," it warned. "Should the 'disappeared' person reappear, the reporters will get into great problems" (*kanabajuutuka*, in Luganda). The pronouncement scared and killed off any fresh reports and follow-ups. It also sent a message to friends and people of goodwill to be careful about visiting families of 'disappeared' people. People believed that there were plain-clothes spies watching our home. Fewer and fewer people came to bring us solace and we felt the grief even more deeply.

While we, in our isolation, hoped, prayed and speculated about William's disappearance, it seemed that many people and the international community in Uganda knew that William had been killed within a day or two of his kidnapping. The first indication of this was two weeks after the abduction in the form of a message from Mrs Pelizolli, the wife of the Air France manager who was renting our house at Tank Hill. "Dear Mrs Kalema," her note said, "I am very sorry about what has happened, but please know that you have your children to live for. Regards, Mrs Pelizolli." The message confirmed my worst fears.

After a while, as I looked at her brief note again, I realised that Mrs Pelizolli's advice and concern gave me much strength. It has held me up to this day as her words, "You have your children to live for …" still echo in my mind. I believe that in Mrs Pelizolli's mind, she thought that she did not have anything to offer me under the circumstances, but in her note, she gave me something valuable and sustaining. I have lived for my children and for their children, since then. May God bless her soul, her husband and their two sons (at that time aged seven and five years), wherever they may be.

Nalubowa, had just turned two when her father was taken from us. A few weeks after he disappeared, she asked me, "*Maama, Taata awuuwa?*" She was trying to say "*Taata aliwa?*" Meaning, "Where is Daddy?" I tried to explain, I cannot remember what I told her.

In my diary, on 18th April 1972, I wrote that after a visit and prayers by some clergymen from Kisugu Church, in Muyenga my daughter Nakibule questioned me persistently. "*Maama*, did *Taata* take any money with him?"

"No," I answered.

"How do you know; did you look in his trouser pocket?"

"Yes."

"And how much money did you find?"

"About 20 shillings."

"Where did he go?"

"I don't know."

"Why?"

"Because he has not written to us."

The next day, 19th April, she resumed her questioning: "Does everybody in the world know that Taata is not here?"

"Not everybody, but our friends know."

"How many, about a hundred?"

"Perhaps more."

"Does the President know that Taata is not here?"

"Yes."

"How do you know? Did you and Taata go to his party?"

"No."

"Why not?"

"Because we were not invited."

The questions were endless and I, too, had many unanswered questions. I sought my answers in prayer as I prayed constantly, alone and with friends who came to comfort me.

That April, an announcement on Radio Uganda stated: "William Wilberforce Kalema left his home and went to an unknown destination." This was probably in response to inquiries from a *Taifa Empya* reporter. By then, I had made three statements to the police and met the Minister for Internal Affairs, Lt. Colonel Ernest Obitre-Gama, in his office. Although he was sympathetic, he seemed uncomfortable. He was clearly helpless. I later learnt that the CID had done their best to investigate my husband's disappearance, but were frustrated by higher powers. So they could not reveal their findings.

William's mother, who had come five weeks earlier to join us and the rest of the family after her son's abduction, returned to her home in Kikoloto, in great despair.

We never stopped searching. We received and welcomed all kinds of information and speculations including those that stated that William could still be alive. Weeks became months and months, years. As I write this, it is now forty-nine years.

The Search for William

Among the people who stood by us as we searched for William, were James Mulwana, Erisa Kironde, and Nelson Sebugwawo. I will relate one of the many endless searches to illustrate the danger and fear that prevailed around that time.

One day, about four months after William's disappearance, through certain channels of inquiry, Nelson Sebugwawo was told about a terrifying place in Nakasongola, towards the northwest, about eighty miles from Kampala, where bodies of kidnapped and murdered people were thrown in bushes. It was a remote, sparsely populated area that was inhabited by small wild animals, herdsmen and their cattle. Sebugwawo decided that we should make yet one more attempt to find William, even if it was only just to recover his friend's bones and give them a decent burial. It was a very secret mission that involved only him, a trusted informer, and myself. Due to the sensitive nature of the mission, we decided that Sebugwawo would drive the 160-miles round trip journey the same day.

When we arrived in the area, we were met by our contact person, a resident who had helped other families search for the remains of their loved ones. He was aware of the danger involved because those who dumped the bodies sometimes left a guard to ensure that no one came to look around. Whenever they brought the bodies, if they found herdsmen around, they would make them lie face down on the ground and fire shots into the air to scare them. That was to ensure that the herdsmen would not be able to identify any person or vehicle or where the bodies were dumped. They would then offload the bodies and drive away. The herdsmen would often lie down for a long time, before getting up and running away with their herds.

We left the car off the road, hidden in a bush, and walked fearfully through the bushes. I remember the guide showed us the remains of a man; some bones without a skull or ribs. The femur and the man's trousers with its waist lining were still intact. The guide informed us that wild animals normally tore away pieces of flesh and bones off the bodies. The pieces from his shirt had not changed colour much and one could still make out the cloth's pattern. The guide asked us what he was wearing on that day. I did not recognise the pieces of cloth, so it was clear he was not William.

We looked around in different places but in the end, found no William. It was a place of great terror and as we made our way quickly to the car, we kept looking back to see if we were being followed. No words can express the devotion and loyalty of Sebugwawo and his family who, for more than seventy years, have meant a lot to our family. They brought a lot of healing to my children and me. We will never forget them.

On 9th August 1972, Idi Amin declared that all non-citizen Asians must leave Uganda within ninety days. Eight days later, on 17th August, he announced that Asian professionals, who were previously exempted from his order, would also be expelled. He had apparently embarked on waging an 'economic war' against the Asians, whom he accused of "sabotaging Uganda's economy and encouraging corruption."

The situation escalated and eventually all Asians with or without Ugandan citizenship were ordered to leave. The expelled Asians lost their homes, factories, farms, shops and other properties and even the few belongings they were allowed to carry with them were confiscated, stolen or destroyed at border crossings and at Entebbe airport.

These gross violations of people's rights affected more than 65,000 people including those whose ancestors had come from South-East Asia at the end of 19th and early 20th Centuries. They had worked hard and settled in Uganda and other Eastern African countries. When they were expelled, they migrated to different parts of the world including, Kenya, India, Pakistan, Bangladesh, UK, USA and Canada, many in humiliating destitution and in great distress.

William had entrusted his will to Mahendra Maini, an Asian friend of his who was a lawyer. He was the younger brother of Sir Amar Maini, the first mayor of Kampala. After Mahendra left Uganda, he went to the UK. He called and told me that he had taken William's will with him for safekeeping but unfortunately, his possessions were confiscated en-route. However, again, by the grace of God, this problem was resolved after a major breakthrough in the law pertaining to missing persons in Uganda.

By 1973, the International Commission of Jurists (ICJ) in Geneva had taken up Uganda's special case of nationals who had disappeared and whose numbers had increased dramatically. The case specially mentioned Chief Justice Benedicto Kiwanuka. A missing person was presumed to be dead if they were not seen for seven years. In response to the pleas of the families of the many people who were killed by government agents, and the lobbying efforts through the Judiciary, the law related to missing persons was amended in Uganda and The Estates of Missing Persons (Management) Act of 1973 reduced the period to three years. Accordingly, my husband was legally declared 'missing, presumed dead' on 12th September 1975, pursuant to Section 20 of the Act. I could now receive my husband's life insurance benefits and rrrr+

obtain letters of administration to allow me to manage his financial affairs and take care of our children.

Following my husband's kidnapping and disappearance, several other former ministers, including Shaban Nkutu, Basil Bataringaya, Alex Ojera and Joshua Wakholi were killed. Other prominent citizens included the Makerere University Vice-Chancellor Frank Kalimuzo, Bank of Uganda Governor Joseph Mubiru, and Chief Justice Benedicto Kiwanuka who were abducted in broad daylight and killed.

Support from Family and Friends

At the beginning, God used family and friends to give us financial and moral support. My brothers, sisters and in-laws, especially my brother Kiwana, helped me in many ways. He bought me two sewing machines so that I could set up a cottage tailoring business, "Kweri Children's Wear", at my home in Nakasero. I employed one lady and we made baby clothes which I sold to clothing stores. We also made girls' uniforms for friends' children who were at the Kitante Primary School with my children. Friends like James Mulwana and Katie Kibuka visited often and brought us food. I will always remember how Sam Rutega, William's Under Secretary in the Ministry of Commerce and Industry, paid Nakibule's whole year's school fees in her Primary Seven.

Mary and Arnold Klopper, and Bishop Cyril Stuart were among the first people who wrote to me. Although they and our other UK friends were a long way away, and we had not met in a long time, they felt very close during that very difficult time. I particularly remember Mary telling me to write about William's life while my memory was still fresh. "Contact people who knew him and request them to write," she advised. I did contact several people who responded but given my emotional state at the time, I found it impossible to concentrate and write about him.

I also received messages of comfort from Nancy Corby in England. Dr Samson Kisekka, a long time friend and member of William's *Mpologama* (lion clan), and his wife Mary Nanfuka Kisekka specially comforted us and I started visiting them regularly. My sister, Janet, who was then the principal of the Lady Irene Teacher Training College in Ndejje, twenty-five miles from Kampala, was once again by my side and her presence made a great difference. She travelled regularly from the college to check on me and we would sleep in the same bed. Her visits lifted my spirits during that very dark period. At one time, she suggested that I go and stay with her for some days in her bungalow that had a beautiful, spacious garden. I obliged and by the time I returned to my house, I felt better and more capable of facing the still very cloudy future.

I received another touching expression of solidarity from the Nagendas. Sala came to visit me with her husband, William, who was quite ill with Parkinson's disease. In spite of this, the love and compassion of the Lord Jesus whom he preached for over thirty-five years was still evident in his loving soul. William told his wife that he wished to deliver his condolences in person.

I was very grateful for the spiritual comfort I received from Reverend Tom Nabeta, the Chaplain of Makerere University, and his wife Julie. Uncle Tom, as he was referred to by my family, came often and prayed with us as he delivered God's message. The visits went a long way in strengthening our spirits.

I was also very comforted when Archbishop Erica Sabiti visited me at home. William and I had attended his consecration service where he was installed as the Bishop of the new Kampala Diocese at All Saints Church, on the 16ᵗʰ of January, just four days before William's disappearance. At the service, the sermon was based on the text from the book of Prophet Isaiah 43: 1-3 (NKJV) "Fear not for I have redeemed you …and through the rivers, they shall not overwhelm you… and through the fire, you shall not be burnt." As I listened to the sermon, I believed that it was meant for the new Archbishop who was about to take on heavy responsibilities. However, I later realised that God was addressing me too.

My God, true to His promise, has been faithful and merciful towards me and my children. Our many, true friends, were a strong 'social capital' for our family. "For I know the plans I have for you," declares the Lord, in Jeremiah 29:11, (NIV) "Plans to prosper you and not to harm you, plans to give you hope and a future." God did indeed give us hope and a future.

The Question of Destiny

I believe that it is hard to debate or argue about 'destiny' because it is a complex concept. So, whether William would have lived longer had he not returned to Uganda when he did, no one can say. I tossed and turned at night with these thoughts on my mind for a long time. But then I believe that since our time and days on this earth are in God's hands, it was God who guided William to return home and die after spending his last days with his family. As Selwyn Hughes put it, "There is a destiny worked out into our beings at the time God created us. We do not produce it, we discover it."[16]

The important thing, I believe, was the value in the plans William made for his family; buying a home in the city centre;

16 Swleyn Hughes, *Every Day with Jesus*, May/June 2005.

and using an insurance policy to improve the house. He planned his children's education and spent quality time with his family in the final eleven months of his life. I have cherished the happy memories of those final moments, especially the last seven and a half months at our Nakasero home. I also believe that this is what gave me the strength to live for our children.

William Kalema was a brave man. Although he sensed that he could not escape the danger, I do not think that he regretted coming back to me, his children, mother and close relatives. He was a selfless, dutiful and conscientious son, husband, father, brother and friend. His return assured us that we had a friend who loved us to the end. Though his body was never found, I was compelled to put on his gravestone these words from John 15:13 (NIV). "Greater love has no one than this: to lay down one's life for one's friends."

* * *

Reflecting on the man I met at Budo, William was a friendly man with an affable manner that earned him many friends. However, those who were close to him knew that he could also be a deeply thoughtful person.

He was reliable and very concerned about other people's wellbeing; he would readily support friends going through dark times, even when he did not have much money. He displayed great determination in everything he did. He combined being supremely confident, focused and farsighted with being organised. At work, newspapers, bits of paper, letters and everything else that required his attention were neatly placed on his desk.

William also had firm convictions. He believed strongly in the African's right to freedom and in justice and equality for all, and that the poor can be lifted out of their poverty. One could argue with him endlessly over these issues. William got the chance to access a good education and he valued it. Indeed, he viewed his education as a challenge for him to create as many educational opportunities as possible for others. Above all, he was devoted to his family.

Forty years after his death, the Kalema family was reunited with Margaret Ritchie who was his personal secretary when he was a government minister. Margaret and her husband, David Ritchie, narrated new stories about William to our children Gladys, Veronica and William Jnr when they met in England. These stories revealed how deeply he treasured his family.

Although my husband's life was cut short at only forty-five years of age, his name, achievements and family have lived on and continued his legacy. I thank God for the twenty-two years we had him in our lives.

Chapter 11

Life After William

Mrs Pelizzoli's advice, that I should live for my children, Betty, William Jr, Peter Martin, Katerega, Nakibule and Nalubowa came in handy. Not long after his father's disappearance, Peter received his 'O' level results. He did very well! I still recall the memory of his agony as he wept bitterly saying, "I would have wanted *Taata* to see these results."

Katerega, who was in his last year at Kitante Primary School, became the head boy that year. One of his teachers, an English lady whose name I cannot recall, confided, "We thought Katerega should be given the responsibility of being the head boy to keep his mind busy." She told me this after asking me, "Does your son know what happened to his father? He does not talk about him." I was touched by their concern. I later realised that his teachers made that decision for his psychological well being. He was the second best pupil in the school in the Primary Leaving Examinations.

After Kitante, Katerega entered King's College Budo for his 'O'level. He was there for three years before moving to Alliance High School in Kikuyu, Kenya to complete his fourth year. For his 'A' level, he joined Lenana High School in Kenya and he was admitted into the London School of Economics (LSE) after that.

Betty graduated in 1974 with a degree in Building Economics (Quantity Surveying). I attended her graduation in Nairobi. After that, she worked at the Multi-Construction Company in Kampala where she really enjoyed her job. I remember her work involved site visits to the new Sir Albert Cook Building at the Mengo Hospital.

William Jnr graduated in 1973 from Emmanuel College, Cambridge University, and he stayed on for a one-year master's degree course. He graduated in 1974. I attended both graduations. It was during his first graduation that I met the Woodsfords who would later have a considerable influence in the writing of this book.

Sue and Peter Woodsford

When I first met Peter and Sue Woodsford, one would have thought that we had been friends for a long time. Between 1963 and 1967 the Woodsfords were teachers at the Busoga College Mwiri, a prominent secondary school in eastern Uganda. They joined the school at different times. They later went to England to get married then they returned to Mwiri after the wedding. They finally returned to Britain for good in 1967 and settled in Cambridge, where Peter had been a student at St John's College, Cambridge University.

It is our son William who first met the Woodsfords through their former student at Mwiri, Daudi Magezi, when he was a student at Southampton University. They proved to be great support for William especially when his father disappeared. It seems that they felt connected to Uganda and their happy memories of Mwiri College were refreshed. The couple and their three children, Bex, Adam and Bridget, became William's second family.

When I went to Cambridge again in 1974 for William's second graduation, I took my youngest daughter, Gladys Nalubowa, who was then four years old, with me. Their daughter Bridget was about the same age and the two little girls developed a strong bond from that time. Peter and Sue loved to travel, and in the early 1980s they linked up with William again in California where he was studying at the California Institute of Technology (Caltech) in Pasadena. We continued to share a lot with them.

It is little wonder then that, years later, once I started seriously considering writing about my life, Peter and Sue became instrumental in getting this book written. Peter took me to task many times on the phone asking, "Rhoda, how is our book?" In 2001, he sent me a postcard whose message ended with, "The challenge now lies with the pen."

In 2008, when they visited Kampala, we arranged to meet so that I could update them on the book's progress. As we sat on the veranda at our mutual friend, Marcella Mukasa's house, where they were staying, Sue gave me a 'plan' on how to go about writing and she also pointed out the important milestones in my life that must be included.

We agreed that in the summer of 2009, I would spend a week at their home in Cambridge going over the book. Fortunately, the planned trip coincided with the birth of my grandson, Samwiri, at the end of July, to Jimmy Byagagaire and Veronica Nakibule. He was born twelve years after his brother, Peter Rwabukye, so his birth was a real blessing to the family.

I spent six days in Cambridge where I had a desk in the Woodsford's study. As I wrote the chapters, Peter sat at his computer and keyed in, edited and finally printed the drafts.

All the while, in the background, Sue happily prepared our meals and did all the chores. The work we did in Cambridge seriously launched a project that had lain dormant since 1988, when I first drafted the first few chapters.

* * *

When William graduated from Cambridge in 1974, he could not return to Uganda due to the difficult political environment that prevailed under Idi Amin's rule. He, therefore, opted to work in the Copper Belt in Zambia as a metallurgical engineer with the Nchanga Consolidated Copper Mines – a joint venture between the Government of Zambia and the Anglo American Corporation.

Later, with the help of Dr Martin Aliker, my year mate at Budo who was also a family friend and mentor to William, and at the time, a dentist in Nairobi, he applied to Caltech in Pasadena. He was accepted in the graduate programme in the Division of Chemistry and Chemical Engineering, in 1978.

Before leaving Cambridge, William arranged for his brother Peter to take a bridging O-level mathematics course in Cambridge in the summer of 1974. Peter then enrolled for an Estate Management course at Reading University from 1974 to 1977. While at Reading, Peter was welcomed by Mary and Arnold Klopper into their home in Aberdeen and, like his brother, William, he received unreserved parental love from the couple during his studies there. On completing his degree, he worked for a well established estate management company in London.

From the age of about six, Gladys Nalubowa developed a great love for pets. Dogs and cats were her favourites. One day, when I returned home for lunch, she reported that Titina, the dog, was very sick and was diarrheaing. When I casually said I would take it to the animal clinic, three hours later at 4 o'clock, she threw herself on the ground yelling, "*Maama* it can die, take it now!" We immediately took Titina to the clinic. Sadly, when we checked in the evening, the dog was dead. I knew that Gladys loved animals, but I had no idea how much and that the passion would determine her career. I have a testimony of deep gratitude to God and to all who made it possible for my youngest child to achieve all she has attained in her life and for her country as a veterinarian and conservationist.

Profound Spiritual Comfort

When William was kidnapped, I experienced a period of profound spiritual testing. The grief and bewilderment were so deep, that I almost lost my fellowship with God completely. Hearing about my situation, Ernest Lohrer sent me comforting messages and texts from the Scriptures. I got interested in reading and learning from spiritual books, including *The Way* by E. Stanley Jones, which I bought in 1972. The Lord also taught me that I needed to pray all the time and that it was important that I support my prayer with Bible texts and promises. I gained a lot of comfort, strength and real trust in God and I was able to comfort my children by transferring to them the hope and trust that I received from the Holy Book. As Psalm 46:10 (NIV) states: "Be still and know that I am God." God helped me accept what I found difficult to understand and taught me how to move on with Him.

I believed in getting hold of any divine string for my survival while reading 'Our Daily Bread' for my devotions, I found out about Silent Unity, a Christian school in Missouri, in America. I opened a prayer relationship with them, asking them to pray for my family. I still recall their letter of 18th

December 1974, which ended with the uplifting words that I needed during that season. They wrote, "Dear Rhoda, Our Christmas prayer for all people is for an awareness of the indwelling love of Christ in every life and every situation – Silent Unity."

* * *

I was gradually stabilising when on 3rd June 1973, my dear brother, Alistaluko Kiwana, died in a car accident. He was very supportive after my husband's death, and his passing at the age of forty-eight was another blow to our family, and of course, to his wife Margaret and their six young children.

In July, Maama Erusa Nalubowa, William's mother also passed away. I was unable to bury her as I had gone to attend William Jnr's graduation. I remember thinking about what she had been through losing her son so tragically. She was a fearless, independent woman and is fondly remembered by the entire family.

Rebuilding our Kiboga Home

In 1974, I discussed the idea of rebuilding our Kiboga home with my two older sons, William and Peter Martin and my husband's cousin, Asafu Kazibwe. They encouraged me to rebuild it and, one day, Kazibwe accompanied me to see what remained of the ruins that were in the midst of overgrown bushes. We wanted to figure out how and where to start.

In early 1975, I approached Barclays Bank for a loan which I expected to pay off with my husband's life insurance policy from the Jubilee Insurance Company. However, due to the circumstances surrounding his death, I was told there was no evidence that he had died and that officially, he had 'disappeared' or was 'a missing person', so there was no definite legal basis to support my claim.

Soon after that, the law changed. In view of the unique circumstances in Uganda, a missing person could be presumed dead after three years. This made it possible for me and many other families to secure letters of administration and probate from the court. I sent the letters to the insurance company in Nairobi, Kenya, for settlement.

Meanwhile, a Barclays Bank official, Mr Iain Knapman, drove with me the 150 miles to and from Kiboga in his car to inspect what remained of our home. He recommended my loan application; it was approved and the money was paid as the claim was being processed.

In March 1975, I embarked on the repairs. Assisted by two family friends, the work was expedited and the costs brought down considerably. Jacob Walugembe offered me his lorry free of charge to ferry building materials from Kampala to Kiboga and James Mulwana, in addition to other concessions, gave me his construction labour team who stayed at the site the entire time working for very reasonable wages. Within six months, our dream home, after four years, was once again habitable.

In October, we held a family thanksgiving and dedication prayer ceremony that was presided over by our local priest, Reverend Nathan Mpanga. I have always believed that the dedication prayer protected our house during the 1981-1986 guerrilla war which gravely affected the entire Kiboga area, which is in the 'Luwero Triangle'. With time, crops thrived, fruit trees produced bountifully and I rekindled my close relationship with the community. This was important especially because I remembered how my husband was dedicated to the people and area.

In 1975, Kiboga County became a functional sub-district with an administrative structure. The new District

Commissioner, Kapswani Chekuto, a progressive young man who had just graduated from Makerere University, was keen on accelerating growth in what he believed was an underdeveloped part of the country that had great potential. One day in 1977, he suggested that I sell my looted and ruined shop building in Kiboga town to the Uganda Commercial Bank so that the bank could establish a branch in the area. He also pointed out that since I only spent a few days every month in Kiboga, I could rent out our home to the bank manager. Chekuto mediated the negotiations with the bank's headquarters in Kampala and within a short time, both proposals were accepted and implemented. Before 1978, there was no bank branch between Kampala and Hoima, 130 miles away. The income from both properties helped me manage the farm on the large piece of land around the house.

There was a big bank opening ceremony and the army band from Masindi graced the occasion. The army men and the public danced to the band music inside our compound during the event. Before long, the bank's presence was felt as it opened up development in Kiboga. Since I had rented out the main house, whenever I was in Kiboga, I spent the day in the small cottage where my faithful gardener, Petero Mpotazi lived. Petero, who fled from his home in Burundi after a genocide, started working for us in 1968 when we employed him as a porter during the first construction of the house. He died in March 2010, after forty-two faithful years with us.

* * *

In 1977, Betty married Godwin Kayondo, her former classmate at Budo, and soon after, they were blessed with their first child, Alice Rhoda Zalwango. They moved to Kenya where Godwin had secured a job. Two years later, they welcomed a son, Juko

Crispus Drake who was born in Nairobi. Betty worked as a quantity surveyor with a number of firms, including Howard Humphreys Consulting Engineers.

She later returned to her alma mater, the University of Nairobi and enrolled for a diploma in computer science. In 1986, armed with her new qualification, she landed a job in the computer department of Shell Uganda. She returned to Kampala with the children while Godwin remained in Nairobi and continued teaching at the university.

In Zambia, William met Felleng Chalale, from Lesotho, and after he enrolled in the graduate programme at Caltech, they got married in 1979. They had their wedding in Nairobi because of the insecurity that prevailed in Kampala after Idi Amin's government was overthrown. Many family members attended the wedding and Felleng and William moved to California after their wedding.

When he completed his studies in 1984, William moved to New Jersey where he worked for Du Pont in the photo products department. Living in East Brunswick, New Jersey, made it possible for him to spend more time with his sister, Veronica Nakibule, who was a student at Princeton University, in the same state.

Chapter 12

Enemy of the State

Idi Amin's chaotic regime ended in 1979, in the same way it had started in 1971: with violence and destruction. Amin was initially welcomed by Ugandans who hoped that his leadership would bring about national unity, but he increasingly became unpopular as his regime changed and started engaging in the repression of citizens. Internationally, Amin was isolated, mainly due to his poor human rights record and his erratic foreign relations policies. His frustrations were meted out on Ugandans.

Professor Samwiri Karugire summarised the situation in the years between 1971 and 1979 in *The Roots of Instability in Uganda*, thus:

> ... every segment of Uganda's population suffered from Amin's random terror: the army, the police, the prison staff, political leaders of every description, public officials and individuals from all walks of life were massacred, all in the name of 'national security'.[17]

However, what probably began the final road towards Amin's downfall was the murder of Archbishop Janani Luwum.

---

17 Samwiri R. Karugire, *The Roots of Instability in Uganda*, p. 80.

The murder, on 17th February 1977, of the Archbishop of Uganda, Janani Jakaliya Luwum, and government ministers, Charles Oboth Ofumbi and Erinayo Wilson Oryema, caused much anguish in Uganda and shocked the whole world.

Archbishop Luwum and his fellow bishops' crime was that they had protested to President Idi Amin about the killings and unexplained disappearances of Ugandans. In response, Amin charged the Archbishop and cabinet ministers with treason and ordered their killing. Many people thronged Namirembe Cathedral to pray for the Archbishop even though his body was not there and there was no funeral or memorial service. His body had been hurriedly taken away by soldiers to his home in Mucwini in northern Uganda and buried the next day after a brief service that was attended by a few relatives and friends.

In March 1976, the Archbishop had attended an Anglican Consultative Council meeting in Trinidad, where he met Bishop Leslie Brown, the first Archbishop of Uganda, who later wrote in his book, *Three Worlds, One Word:*

> I had asked Janani about the outcome of the tyranny in Uganda. He had replied: 'We have to stand for the truth and some of us may be killed. But we are in God's hands so we do not fear'.[18]

Archbishop Luwum is recognised as a martyr by the Church of England and the Anglican Communion. His death is marked on February 17th, as a Lesser Festival and his statue is among those of the 20th Century martyrs in front of Westminster Abbey, in London. February 16th is a public holiday in Uganda that commemorates his life and service to the country.

---

18 Leslie Brown, *Three Worlds, One Word* (London: Rex Collings, 1981), p. 234

Arrested

By January 1979, threatened by war, Idi Amin continued to agressively look for enemies within Uganda – both real and imaginary. I got caught up: the regime believing that I was one of its deadly enemies.

A former business partner of mine, Robert Sebunya, was suspected of fighting Amin from Nairobi. As Amin's agents investigated him, they discovered his connection with a paper clip company, Manufacturing Stationers Ltd, which he had started with my husband and Basil Dungu. They concluded that the shareholders and directors – Basil Dungu and I – were Sebunya's political accomplices and our arrest was ordered.

Basil was arrested first. For two days, he refused to reveal my whereabouts. I was informed about his arrest by office staff who told me that I was also wanted. I kept away from the office and my home and went to stay with James and Sarah Mulwana. However, since I knew that my mother who lived with me was alone and worried, I decided to return home and wait for them. On the morning of 23rd January 1979, at about 11 a.m., the SRB agents came for me; it was exactly seven years and three days after my husband was abducted.

The agents came to my home on Nakasero Road with Basil. He did not talk to me but I could tell that he was being held captive. I was placed in the back seat with him while two tall, dark Nubian men sat in front. Basil indicated to me, using sign language, that he had had no option but to tell them where my house was.

We were taken to the SRB headquarters, which was referred to as the 'Devil's Den'. It was opposite All Saints Cathedral, in Nakasero. There, Basil and I sat in an office for about three hours, waiting, watched by two giggling secretaries who were excited about the capture of 'prisoners'. We were not allowed to talk, so we communicated using our eyes. We were given some food and while I managed to eat a little, Basil did not. Shortly afterwards, he was taken away and I never saw him again.

As night fell, at about seven o'clock, I was called into the office of the 'Technical Operations Officer'. He gave me a piece of paper and a pen and asked me to write a statement about my company's business, including what I knew of my partners. After handing him my statement, the officer told me that a partner in my company was outside Uganda causing 'problems' for the government. He added that they were satisfied that I was not involved in his activities and that I should forget him. He then told me that I would be taken back to my house that night. I must say that I did not have any faith in the statement. At 10 o'clock though, I was placed in the same small saloon car that picked me up that morning and driven back home under the guard of the same big, tall Nubian man. Although it was less than a five minutes' drive, it seemed like a very long journey. On the way, the guard advised me not to attempt to escape from the country. "Because, you know, even if you run away, you can die," he warned. I later learnt that it was Gordon Wavamunno, a prominent businessman and family friend, who convinced the SRB to release me.

Meanwhile, the enemies Amin had fretted about during his eight-year rule, were crossing into Uganda at the Mutukula border. At the end of March, in spite of the warning, as the war approached Kampala, I escaped. My friends, James Mulwana and Gordon Wavamunno smuggled me to Nairobi. Gordon, who had established Spear Motors as the sole Mercedes Benz dealer in the country, requested and received the government's permission to take his Mercedes Benz car to Nairobi, the only place it could be serviced. I left with a driver. At this time, all my children were living outside Uganda including the last three who were schooling in Kenya. My children, friends and relatives were very concerned about me and among my beliefs about this difficult time is that God brought our dear family friends to my aid so that I could live to tell this tale.

I had many family members in Nairobi and I stayed with my sister Gladys and her husband, Justice Wako Wambuzi, who was working at the Kenya Court of Appeal. They lived near my brother, Dr Semu Nsibirwa and his wife Edisa. When I left for Nairobi, James and Sarah Mulwana moved my mother to their home in Kansanga, a suburb of Kampala.

The Moshi Conference

In October 1978, Amin had attacked the Kagera Salient, an area north of the Kagera River in north-western Tanzania, wreaking havoc and killing Tanzanian civilians, destroying property and livestock and effectively annexing the territory. President Julius Kambarage Nyerere of Tanzania had responded to the provocation by mobilising the Tanzania People's Defence Force (TPDF) and mounting a retaliatory intense counteroffensive a few weeks later which caused Ugandan troops to retreat and Amin to retract his territorial claims.

The Tanzanian troops then joined the thousands of anti-Amin Ugandan refugees who had constituted themselves into a fighting force. Although President Nyerere had declared that Tanzania had no intention of occupying any part of Uganda, the combined forces launched a major offensive in late January 1979 with the aim of overthrowing Amin's regime.

In late February, the town of Masaka was taken, cutting off any support that Amin would have received from his battalion west of Masaka. In mid-March, the offensive faced and routed Libyan troops that had been deployed to save Amin's regime in the Battle of Lukaya. The devastation of the troops cleared all obstacles in the combined army's advance towards Kampala.

Sensing imminent success and the subsequent collapse of Amin's regime, President Nyerere brought together disparate and fractious anti-Amin groups and charted out a post-Amin Uganda to prevent the possibility of a political vacuum. The groups consisted of Ugandan exiles mainly from Tanzania, Kenya, Zambia, and as far away as Europe and the United States. He hosted a 'unity' conference of around 200 people from twenty-two organisations, in Moshi, northern Tanzania, in March 1979.

The participants adopted the 'Moshi Spirit of Unity' and created an umbrella body called the Uganda National Liberation Front (UNLF). It had a military wing – the Uganda National Liberation Army (UNLA) – under the leadership of General Tito Okello and Brigadier David Oyite-Ojok.

UNLF participants composed themselves into a National Consultative Council (NCC) which became the governing body of the UNLF, under the chairmanship of Professor Edward Rugumayo. The Council then elected a National Executive Committee (NEC). Professor Yusuf Kironde Lule, was appointed Chairman of the NEC and was therefore poised to be the president once Uganda was liberated. Lule, an academecian, had been the Principal of Makerere College and the Assistant Secretary General of the Commonwealth Secretariat in London. In their book, *War in Uganda*, Tony Avirgan and Martha Honey state that Lule:

… had not been an important exile leader, but in the crucial weeks before the Moshi Conference, some quick and careful groundwork had been done in London, Nairobi and Dar es Salaam to prepare the path for his rise to prominence. His credentials made him an ideal compromise candidate, capable of uniting Ugandans internally and externally.[19]

The UNLF created a Military Commission to oversee its military affairs. It comprised of people from the frontline. It was chaired by Paulo Muwanga and Yoweri Museveni was the Vice Chairman. General Tito Okello and Brigadier Oyite-Ojok were also members of the Commission. It is important to note that Milton Obote, who was ousted by Amin, was left out of all leadership positions and he remained in Dar es Salaam.

The Fall of Kampala

I was still in Nairobi on 11ᵗʰ April 1979, when the UNLF and the Tanzanian army, the TPDF, overthrew Amin's regime. On 13ᵗʰ April, Yusuf Lule was sworn in as President of Uganda by the re-appointed Chief Justice, Samuel Wako Wambuzi, who returned to Kampala as soon as Amin was overthrown. I travelled to Kampala with him on the same small plane.

The UNLF called themselves 'liberators' and were believed to be the new hope for the country. People danced with jubilation in the streets, relieved, that after eight long years, the terror was over. With the fall of Kampala, people also poured into the city, looting anything they could lay their hands on. Shops, homes, government offices, stores, everything was ransacked and the loot was carried away in broad daylight.

19 Tony Avirgan and Martha Honey, *War in Uganda: The Legacy of Idi Amin* (Dar es Salaam: Tanzania Publishing House, 1983), p. 106.

The good Lord used my housekeeper Jackson, who was alone at home in Nakasero, to save my house from being looted. Seeing a crowd of looters and soldiers amassing in front of the house, he got hold of my late husband's portrait and waved it at the Tanzanian soldiers. "Idi Amin killed this Minister, Kalema," he shouted at them. "This was his house!" The instant reaction of the soldiers was to guard my house and they sent away the looters. A few of them must have remembered that 'Kalema' was the name of one of Amin's early victims.

My house was one of the few that escaped looting in our area. My sister Dr Rosemary and her husband, Dr Edward Kigonya's house, was looted and left completely bare. Their wedding photograph was picked up in the middle of the road near their house by one of their patients. It was the only momento from their home that remained. Many people lost their possessions and important documents in the chaos. The best thing about our fortunate escape from the looting was that our personal records were saved, especially photographs and albums. I shall always be thankful to Jackson. It is however sad that I have lost any hope of ever meeting him again on this earth. He went back to his home in Kabale in south-western Uganda in 1979 and I never heard from him again. May God bless his soul!

When the UNLF finally reached Kampala, they knew that Uganda no longer had a parliament because Amin, who ruled by decree, abolished it in 1971. The NCC, therefore, became the interim legislature that deliberated on behalf of the people.

However, soon there were signs that the UNLF government could not function properly and it was almost guaranteed to fail. As Prof. Karugire observes in *The Roots of Instability in Uganda*:

> To begin with, since all institutions of government had been manned by Amin's personal appointees, these ceased to exist once Amin fell. Thus, the UNLF government had no police, army, judiciary, civil service or chiefs. All these had to be built from scratch and yet the team which was supposed to do this building was itself hopelessly divided without any sense of cohesion or direction. Very soon, 'liberation' became a nightmare for the people of Uganda as lawlessness mounted and government appeared powerless to contain it.[20]

Take-off for the new government was not smooth. Several changes quickly took place among the top leadership. Apparently, the Moshi arrangements had vested more power in the NCC and Military Commission than in the President, so when President Lule failed to agree with the NCC, he was removed – after only 68 days in office. He was replaced by Godfrey Binaisa, but within a year, he too was removed by the Military Commission.

After the change of government in April 1979, Katerega, who was nineteen years old, went to Amin's former army headquarters, Republic House (it was originally known, by 1966, as *Bulange* and was the home of the Buganda parliament) to find out if there were any records on his father's death. Unfortunately, he did not find any. He only told me about

---

20 Karugire, *The Roots of Instability in Uganda*, p. 73.

the visit later. He had been particularly close to his father and although he had been old enough at eleven to miss his father, he was not able to make sense of the political conflicts that could have led to his disappearance. From the incident (looking for the records), I realised that he had never really come to terms with his father's death. This must have contributed to his mental confusion and ultimately, depression.

Chapter 13

Getting Involved in Politics and Government

The decision to involve myself in politics was, on the face of it, puzzling: how and why would I get involved in politics after losing my husband to its dangers? I struggled with this question and imagined that it was also on the mind of many people. At the time of Uganda's independence in 1962, I did not aspire to join politics, but my husband's political life must have triggered some interest in me. When Adoko Nekyon and Grace Ibingira, staunch members of the UPC, convinced me to join their party in 1963, I had already been inspired by the nationalist views of the party. However, my support for the party and its government was shattered by the incident of 24th May 1966, in which the Uganda Army attacked Kabaka Mutesa II at his palace and forced him to flee into exile.

The situation was now different. I wished to see if I could make a difference by contributing to peace and sane governance in a country where my children and grandchildren would grow up and live. I did not want to be a mere spectator when there was a real possibility that my country could slide back into chaos similar to what we had experienced under Idi Amin. Bad leadership, coupled with impunity, had cost the lives of so many sons and daughters of Uganda. The economy and infrastructure were destroyed and many people forced into exile.

Under the UNLF government, membership of the interim parliament, the NCC, was at first confined to those who had joined as fighters or liberators. However, they soon realised that they needed to include citizens like me who had been in the country for eight years under Amin in the interim parliament and government. They called us, the 'stayees'. The NCC was opened up to new members and the big districts were allowed to elect three nominees, and the small ones, two. When people were invited to fill in a simple nomination application form in their respective districts, I got interested.

A member of the Kampala District Council, James Mulwana, who knew about my political concern and interest in the new set-up asked me if I wished to apply. As I had a home in Kampala, I decided to apply through the Kampala District. Together with Henry Kayondo and Dent Ocaya Lakidi, I was nominated to represent Kampala. We set out to find out what the people of Kampala needed the most. We found out that there were hardly any social services in the capital, and that we had a giant task before us.

One of the projects involved the creation of a clean water access point at Kyebando, a suburb on Gayaza Road. We planned, with the people in the area, the cleaning up of a natural spring and, eventually, the newly widened spring produced clean water. It was a difficult task but it excited the citizens, many of whom were seeing their representatives for the first time. They were very impressed and happy that through their own hard work, they had clean water. It seemed that the nominees to the NCC were more accountable to the people than the 'liberators' in the original NCC because the 'stayees' understood the prevailing situation on the ground better.

Although I was an official representative for Kampala District, I also made every effort to get essential supplies to the people of Kiboga, including sugar, salt, soap and even clothing that had become very scarce and expensive. There had been many killings in the rural areas and the government administration had weakened. I realised that the miserable situation that existed in the city prevailed in Kiboga as well.

Deputy Minister Appointment

The new batch of representatives was sworn in during August 1979. Soon after, I was appointed Deputy Minister for Culture and Community Development. Dani Wadada Nabudere, a liberator, was the senior minister.

As Deputy Minister, I concentrated on the revival of community clubs and centres that existed in rural areas before independence and under the first post-independence government. The facilities around then had permanent community development officers attached to them and had been of great value to adult education and recreation. I even tried to get some television sets for the clubs from the Ministry of Information. Although the Minister, Akbar Adoko Nekyon, seemed keen on my proposal, I never got the sets.

A few months after my appointment, the government, under Godfrey Binaisa, sent a cultural troupe to entertain and thank the Government of Tanzania and the TPDF for their contribution to the liberation war. Nabudere and I accompanied the troupe to Dar-es-Salaam. In the letter we carried, the NCC said it had no better way of thanking the Tanzania people for the sacrifice they had made to uproot Amin's regime, than by sending a troupe. We got an enthusiastic reception.

Breakdown of the 'Moshi Spirit of Unity'

At the beginning of 1980, President Godfrey Binaisa, was ousted and the Military Commission replaced him with a Presidential Commission of three retired judges – Saulo Musoke, Joel Hunter Wacha-Olwol, and Polycarp Nyamuconco. Paulo Muwanga, the Chairman of the Military Commission, became the *de facto* head of government. It was clear that the 'Moshi Spirit of Unity' was breaking down in the NCC. The old political parties had quietly regrouped and the UPC group was determined to regain power. Although he was the Vice-chairman of the Military Commission, Yoweri Museveni was too powerless to stop the UPC's plans to return Milton Obote to power.

The UPC plan was accomplished on 27th May 1980 when Milton Obote landed on an airfield near Mbarara Town in western Uganda. From there, he travelled to Bushenyi, thirty-five miles further west where he was offered a grand reception. Straightaway, his return to Uganda resurrected the old conflicts surrounding the UPC, and the disagreements between the exiled groups in Moshi resurfaced.

While serving in the NCC, I learnt more about the Moshi Conference, the twenty-two political groups that had met there and the two fundamental Moshi decisions that were arrived at. First, a general election was to be held two years after Amin was overthrown to allow enough time for proper preparations to be made for meaningful adult suffrage. Second, elections were to be held under the umbrella of the UNLF and the candidates were to be voted for based on merit, not on political party affiliations. These two considerations were arrived at in an attempt to heal political wounds as efforts were made to rebuild the country.

Despite the sensitivity of the Moshi decisions, by June 1980, it was clear that the UPC group had decided not to abide by the resolutions. The NCC decided to revisit the resolutions and a heated debate, which lasted three weeks, ensued on whether to move the election date forward to December 1980, and carry it out based on political parties. I remember there was an actual physical division of people when the issue was put to vote. Those in favour of waiting two years before elections and voting under one umbrella were forty-eight, against fourteen. However, a day later, it was announced on radio that the "UPC has decided to contest the elections as UPC" and "DP has decided to contest as DP." Both parties had apparently agreed to hold the elections in December. The UPC believed it had the military might to do what they wanted, and the DP trusted that it had the numbers to win.

There was fear that Uganda would slide back into turmoil as those with military power would stop at nothing to gain political supremacy. Many people, including myself, were of the opinion that reviving political parties so soon would disrupt the country before it had recovered fully. A split was, therefore, inevitable.

The Uganda Patriotic Movement

I decided to join a group that was opposed to the revival of political parties so soon. We decided to form an alternative political organisation – the Uganda Patriotic Movement (UPM). The idea of a 'movement' denoted unity and communicated that the main drive behind the formation of the new party was patriotism and the love for our country. The other founders of the movement were Eriya Katègaya, Jaberi Bidandi Ssali, Reverend Father Christopher Okoth, Matia Kasaija, Kirunda Kivejinja, Erisa Kironde, and Aloysious Bakulumpagi. I was involved in the original discussions, absolutely convinced that Ugandans needed guidance on how to remain united during that sensitive period, for the sake of rebuilding the country.

Although initially he was not committed, Yoweri Museveni joined us later. In fact, Museveni was not our first choice for consideration as UPM's leader. We first considered Akena p'Ojok, before we learnt that he had been discouraged and pulled away by Milton Obote and Paulo Muwanga. That was when we picked Museveni. It is true that while Museveni did not like the idea of joining any of the old parties, he was not keen on our new group either. However, we felt that he was the only suitable alternative. Later, he was convinced that our new proposal was right and he finally accepted to become the UPM leader in the planned general elections of 10th December, 1980.

We registered UPM in August 1980 – three months to the elections. The group was small and had nothing except a belief that our ideas were right for the country. That was, indeed, patriotism. We were sure of what we wanted and what we did not want. We stuck steadfastly to our beliefs and purpose.

At first, we either met in different members' offices or at the Kampala City Council. After some time, we rented office space; a small room on Kampala Road, above a stationery shop that belonged to my sister Eseza, Erisa Kironde's wife. Three key obstacles faced us as we embarked on setting up structures and keeping the party going. First, we did not have financial resources. Second, there was a lack of popular understanding and knowledge – the people did not understand what UPM was all about. Third, was the formidable UPC group of Milton Obote, Paulo Muwanga, and Oyite Ojok.

Money was a major obstacle. Funds were needed especially for transport, maintaining the new office, getting staff, making posters and setting up meetings with the small groups within Kampala. Furthermore, we needed to reach people right across the country with our message. Responding to our very strong insistence, the Electoral Commission gave us one small two-door Toyota pickup, to assist us with our nationwide campaigns. Although the UPC and DP received more vehicles, we were determined to do our best with our meagre resources.

People's scepticism and lack of confidence in UPM made our task even harder. Many people, when addressed, would say dismissively, "We are tired of political parties." When we told them about our sixteen aims and objectives that focused on unity, democracy, clean leadership and peace, they would ask: "But where can this new party take us?"

Campaigning at the Grassroots

Despite overwhelming obstacles, we were determined to reach the grassroots. I gave myself the task of personally campaigning in Kiboga. I talked to the people about UPM and tried to convince them that the 'movement' was for all those who were tired of the old political parties. Young people, in particular, seemed to like our ideas.

In November 1980, two weeks before the elections, I held a rally with Matia Kasaija in Kiboga. We travelled in the Toyota pickup from the Electoral Commission. We had by then printed local Nytil fabrics in the party colours of blue, green, red and white – a merger of UPC and DP colours. We made gowns, shirts and dresses. In Kiboga we placed banners and paper flags with our colours all over the town alongside our new slogan, 'Clean Leadership, Unity and Peace'.

At the rally in Kiboga trading center, Matia Kasaija and I turned out in our party gowns and we were received with great excitement. Many shops closed as people flocked to listen to our message. We told them that those who were tired of the ideologies of the old parties could start on a new road by becoming members of UPM. As we campaigned, we felt that we were bringing the right message to the people at the right time. We were encouraged by the receptiveness of the people to our message. We returned to Kampala, tired but in high spirits.

Makerere University students were also attracted to our UPM message. Our slogan was particularly popular at the university and converted members went about recruiting fellow students. A group of students invited UPM officials to the campus one evening for a meeting in the Mary Stuart dining hall. It was full of boisterous students. Aloysius Bakulumpagi, a former lecturer at Makerere who had recently returned to Uganda after working in Kenya, was also present. He did a lot of work to attract students to UPM.

I tried to introduce UPM to church leaders so that they could influence their flock. We were not going to leave anyone behind! One morning, I went to see Bishop Misaeri Kawuma in his office at Namirembe, taking with me pamphlets of the UPM manifesto. He was polite and showed interest in any new idea that could stop another UPC government. However, he was not comfortable about Christians supporting a party that was led by Museveni, whom he believed to be a 'communist'. Christians knew communist governments to be intolerant of religion. He was also worried about my spiritual life as the Christian he knew me to be. I tried to convince him that Museveni was not a communist, but as the election results showed later, I did not succeed. Almost all the Anglican churches in Uganda were advised by their leaders to vote for DP since it was strongly associated with the Roman Catholic Church. We later learnt that people believed and were saying, "At least the Christian faith will be certain to survive with Paulo Kawanga Semwogerere (the DP leader), than with Museveni".

When the election date was finally fixed, I vied for Kiboga West on the UPM ticket. I knew my chances of winning were slim, but I pressed on. My standing against UPC, our former party (with my husband), angered Dr Obote. I later learnt that a scheme had been hatched to ambush and kidnap me on the nomination day to give advantage to my opponent. It was only through God's grace that I escaped being kidnapped.

On that day, I did not travel from Kampala. Instead, I travelled from Kiboga where I had spent the night to Mubende District headquarters, where the nominations were being held. Unaware of any danger, I was endorsed as the candidate for Kiboga West.

I discovered the 'kidnap plot' when I returned home to Kampala. My mother gave me a note from a UPM supporter called Mr Kiku. It warned that I should not take the Sekanyonyi or Mityana routes to Mubende from Kampala. He had feared for my safety but had no other way of warning me. My mother and family were greatly relieved when I returned safely to Kampala. No wonder that one key UPC supporter and candidate was visibly shocked when I arrived at the headquarters for the nomination.

In spite of the many obstacles, I succeeded in reaching out to my supporters and mobilising a large number of young men who joined UPM. Many voters in Kiboga told me that they would only vote for me if I vied under DP. I explained to them my deep belief that none of the traditional political parties should be considered at that moment, and why. My sentiments were the same for the other newcomer party, the Conservative Party (CP), which had no national political objective that could rebuild the country.

Before the elections, it was noted that there were many glaring malpractices that were carried out by the UPC. Some of my young supporters in Kiboga were persecuted and a number of them later joined Museveni in the rebellion that began in February, 1981. Almost forty years later, Sam Waswa is still serving as a senior officer in the national army, the UPDF.

During the elections, there was violence and massive vote-rigging. Immediately after the elections, the Chairman of the Military Commission, Paulo Muwanga, took over the role of the Electoral Commission and declared it illegal for anyone to announce results without his approval. He warned that anyone who contravened the order would be arrested. DP's John Bosa was the victor in Kiboga West and he was one of the few DP winners who were rightfully declared winners. The UPC candidate was second and I was last, with 1,350 votes. In most constituencies, UPC candidates were falsely declared winners. Generally, it was believed that the DP won the general elections. The only UPM candidate who won a seat was Dr Crispus Kiyonga in Kasese. However, he immediately fled into exile.

After the elections, the UPC formed a new government with Dr Apollo Milton Obote as President, and the DP formed the opposition in Parliament. Thus, Obote began his second term as President in a tenure that was to score dismally in its human rights record and pillage.

Challenging the Election Results

UPM considered going to court over the rigged election. We accepted that UPM had come last, but we believed that DP won the elections, not UPC. Our young UPM member, Aloysius Bakulumpagi, and another member ventured to be the main plaintiffs. However, the case never made it to court.

Aloysius Bakulumpagi deserves a special mention in this book. He was among the first UPM activists who were arrested after the elections. His father had been shot and killed by Amin's soldiers in 1976. Aloysius was abducted from his home in front of his family and neighbours on 26th March 1981, after a soldier ordered him to lie down. He later recorded:

> I do so immediately and the soldiers begin to stab me with their bayonets, rifle butts, and to kick me with their military boots. Somebody among the residents, probably my wife, screams. Children and women begin screaming and crying. I am bleeding profusely, but have not begun to feel any pain. The stabbing, butting and boot kicks continue for what seems to me like an eternity… Four men grab me by the limbs and throw me, as you would a sack of dry beans, on to a white Datsun 1200 pick-up van. One soldier stands with his heavy boots on my swollen head, another stands on my stomach while a third stands over my thighs. Bleeding intensifies. I can feel it.[21]

---

[21] Human Rights violation in Uganda under Obote by Yususf Lule: Munger African Library Notes, Issue 67, November 1982 California Institute of Technology p. 16-17

An examination revealed that a bayonet stab had missed his heart by a fraction of an inch; the kicks had dislocated a rib and his spleen was damaged. Worse was to come. He ended up being tortured and imprisoned at Makindye Military Barracks where he spent two-and-a-half weeks in filthy cells, hearing and seeing people being tortured, shot and bludgeoned to death. He recalled:

> Each of those days was a day waiting for death, a day of hunger, and a day of witness to untold human suffering. Above all, each day was a day of degradation and dehumanisation. A total of between 25 and 30 inmates were killed in those two-and-a-half weeks I was in Makindye – that is from Death Cell alone.

Bakulumpagi managed to escape from the barracks and he later fled into exile, to Canada. After the National Resistance Movement (NRM) took power in 1986, he returned home. One morning, at Fairway Hotel in Kampala, I bumped into him – a lucky meeting, as he was travelling back to Canada the next day. I can never forget the joy and excitement of our meeting after six years. I remember putting into his hands all the little cash I had in my handbag, my inadequate gift at the joy of meeting again, remembering his courage and all he went through.

Sadly, soon after, Bakulumpagi developed a serious illness in one of his organs. He was flown home but he died shortly after at Rubaga Hospital. He was only in his early forties. I attended his funeral in Buwama, in Mawokota, on Masaka Road. President Yoweri Museveni also attended the funeral of this gallant young son of Uganda.

When I went to Montreal, Canada, in June 1991 for a First World Summit whose theme was 'Women and the Many Dimensions of Power', Joseph Tomusange, the Ugandan High Commissioner, gave me directions to Bakulumpagi's family home and I visited his wife Florence and her children. Bakulumpagi's ordeal was one of the first in a series of crackdowns on political activists that characterised Obote's regime of which I, too, was a victim.

The story of Aloysius Bakulumpagi illustrates the sacrifice and heavy cost a country pays when it is badly governed. Patriotism was our driving force in UPM. I still believe that patriotism, spoken or unspoken, must be the base for peace and progress in any country. It cannot be forced, legislated or taught in class; it can only be learned through developing a tradition of good governance that cares for all the citizens and makes everyone feel that their country is their home. As Edmund Burke (1729-1797), an Irish orator, philosopher and politician rightly stated, "To make us love our country, our country ought to be lovely."

* * *

The tensions of the past two years eased a little after the elections and people were trying to resume their daily routines. I was unaware, at the start of January 1981, of the many developments that were taking place around the country.

One of the developments was that Museveni made good on his threat of staging resistance against the rigged elections. He had publicly vowed to do so and he was preparing to 'go to the bush' to fight the government. The other was that the UPC government had started persecuting prominent members of the UPM. The storm was just about to break.

At the end of January 1981, I visited Kiboga where I spent a night before returning to Kampala on 1ˢᵗ February. Five days later, on the night of 6ᵗʰ February 1981, Museveni's armed group attacked the Kabamba Military Training School in Mubende. The story was that, coming through Kiboga town, which is about eighty miles from Kabamba, Museveni's group raided the police post, 'borrowed' guns and signed for them. In his book, *Sowing the Mustard Seed*, Museveni states that he addressed a small rally in Kiboga town causing great excitement among the newly sensitised UPM youth. He then disappeared into the bush. Many young people decided to follow him.[22]

My house was adjacent to the police post and the UPM connection to Museveni made me a prime suspect as I was falsely associated with the rebellion. The government was convinced that my house must have been the base for the raid. What followed a few days later, was, therefore, not surprising.

---

22 Yoweri Museveni, *Sowing the Mustard Seed: The Struggle for Freedom and Democracy in Uganda* (London: Macmillan, 1997), p. 125.

Chapter 14

Arrests and Imprisonment

My arrest was effected almost immediately. I had just heard about the start of the rebellion in Kiboga on the government radio station on 10th February 1981. On the night of 12th February, just after eight o'clock, my gardener entered the house, looking very frightened. He said that there were people outside and, as he was speaking, a man holding a pistol entered.

"Are you Mrs. Kalema?" he barked. I admitted that I was.

"Sit down, all of you," he said, pointing his pistol at my mother and myself. This frightened my mother greatly. The man disconnected the telephone cable immediately and ordered me into my bedroom. He was looking for guns, so he said. After rummaging around my wardrobe for a few minutes and finding none, he got hold of my two briefcases. He then ordered me to follow him out of the house. I left just as I was, wearing bedroom slippers. My old mother was left in the house with my late husband's nephew, Dan Ndaula.

Outside the gate, we boarded a pickup truck. I sat between the 'arresting agents', the gunman and the soldier who was driving the vehicle. I later learnt that the gunman was called Tom Masaba and that he was a member of the National

Security Agency (NASA), the regime's intelligence service. NASA had just been formed specifically to gather intelligence on any emerging subversions and to deal with rebels and their collaborators. It had replaced the National Security Service (NSS), which had replaced Idi Amin's SRB.

The pickup immediately took off at a very high speed and within minutes, we arrived at the Nile Hotel (now the Kampala Serena Hotel), where top government offices and security operations were based. Masaba went into the hotel and when he came back after some time, proceeded to question me. He wanted me to admit that I had attended Museveni's rally in Kiboga the previous week. I denied it because genuinely I did not know anything about Museveni addressing a rally in Kiboga or anywhere else. Masaba then threatened to show me a photograph taken of me at the rally and I agreed to see it.

"Anyway, it does not matter very much," he said when his bluff failed.

He got into another car and drove off alone very fast, towards Parliament Avenue, firing his gun in the air as he went – most likely to scare me.

At about 1.00 a.m., a young soldier took Masaba's place in the vehicle. A woman colleague of theirs who wanted a lift to the Apolo Hotel (now the Sheraton Hotel), entered and sat on my lap for the distance. Another pickup I saw being loaded with guns joined us. The two vehicles set off on what I believed would be a fatal journey for me.

Just before we left the gate of the hotel, a piece of old cloth, torn off an army uniform, was pulled from the back of the driver's seat and tied over my eyes. Blindfolded, I believed that I was going to be killed anytime.

"Where are you taking me?" I asked.

"We are taking you to a place where you will get a good rest," replied the driver.

I recited Psalm 23 loudly. The driver warned me, "Stop that or you will be in more trouble." In spite of this, I continued speaking out all the six verses of the Psalm.

"Please do not torture me or kill me," I remember saying to the driver and the guard. "I have children who are the same age as you and one day, you may come across them." Neither responded.

They drove to several places and stopped twice. At the first stop, we entered a gate and the driver said to the gateman in Kiswahili, "*Tutarudi saa hii*! (We will return immediately)", as he opened the gate. They drove for some distance before stopping. The driver and some people from the car behind us got out of the vehicles. They held a long discussion but since I was still blindfolded, I could only hear murmurs. They then entered the vehicles and we drove out of the gate.

Another discussion was held at a second stop. This must have been by a roadside as I could hear the kind of noises insects and small animals make at night. As I learned later, they could have been defying orders from the top. Knowing that many people were killed during Amin's regime in similar circumstances – Thereza Nanziri, the warden of Africa Hall at Makerere University and brilliant mathematician came to mind – I owe my survival solely to God's mercy. I believe He had special plans for me which include telling this tale.

Finally, at around 6.00 a.m., we arrived at what I found out later was the Katabi Army Barracks in Entebbe. I was left in the car (still blindfolded) and when they returned, I was driven to two other places which I believed were within Entebbe. At around 8.00 am, the dirty blindfold was removed. After the many hours of total darkness, it felt like I was looking into a bright furnace.

I realised that we were at another military barracks, one that was still under Tanzania's TPDF, which had stayed on in Uganda after Idi Amin was overthrown.

I was taken to the administration office where I was questioned. Apparently, my offence was that I was 'Museveni's sister' and I was cooking for his guerrillas in the bush.

"They have brought in Museveni's sister," the TPDF soldiers called out to each other as they came to view 'this dangerous relative of Museveni'! Two young soldiers believed it and they were really angry with me. "We left our parents and families to come and save Uganda from Idi Amin and now you are fighting us," they said, pointing guns at me.

Just then, a Tanzanian officer, Major Sakapala, alerted about Museveni's sister being in the barracks, entered. He recognised me, but he did not indicate or show that he had any interest in me.

I, too, recognised Major Sakapala. During the fall of Kampala in April 1979, when Jackson, my housekeeper, defended my house on Nakasero Road from looters, soldiers were stationed at my house to provide security. Major Sakapala was among the top Tanzanian army officers in charge of Kampala around then and he lived near us on Nakasero Road. When I joined the NCC at the end of 1979, we became good friends. He would sometimes visit me and he introduced his wife to me when she visited Kampala from Tanzania. Therefore, Major Sakapala and I were well acquainted.

When he returned to his office, he must have asked that

they stop insulting me because they ceased immediately. Major Sakapala's attitude was an indication of Tanzanian forces' perspective towards the emerging conflict. One could see that many of the top TPDF officers were not satisfied with the way the general election had been conducted. Perhaps they understood that Museveni's bush war was a consequence of the rigged election results and an unjust government.

Before long, I was driven back to the Katabi Barracks. There, I was led into a building where I was ordered to sit on a very cold cement floor. Fortunately, again by God's grace, I was wearing the long dress I had on when I was arrested from my home the previous evening. Since Idi Amin's regime had decreed that women should only wear long dresses and skirts known as 'maxis', I had plenty of them. The dress protected my legs from the cold to some extent.

At Katabi Barracks, I found several UPM members and other people who had been arrested, including Jaberi Bidandi Ssali and Byaruhanga Akanga, a soldier. I was soon joined by another woman, Joyce, who worked at the Entebbe Airport control tower. She was accused of spying for UPM and Bidandi Ssali, but she told me she did not know him. We were given some canned pineapples and biscuits which were welcome. This was the 13th of February 1981, and we were the only two women prisoners in the barracks.

In the afternoon, we faced an interrogation committee that included many notorious officers from the police, other security organs, and NASA. Also present were Major Sakapala and another Tanzanian officer. Altogether, there were nine interrogators sitting in a horseshoe formation. We were interviewed separately. Some questions were very annoying and cruel. Others did not make much sense, I did not see how they could help them gather evidence. One question was, "But did you not know that Museveni said he would go to the bush?"

"Yes," I replied, "I know he said so, but I did not believe he would do it." In spite of what I thought was my evident innocence, they decided to keep me in prison.

Joyce and I were taken to a room where it appeared we were to stay, indefinitely. We were given two old two inch thick mattresses and two very thin blankets. The following day, two more women joined us. After two more days, we were five. Margaret, Joyce, Sophie, Nalongo, and I. We shared the two school-size mattresses and two thin blankets. The room, once a food store, was adjacent to the barrack's beans, rice and maize meal (*posho*) store. The beans bred a lot of weevils, which freely walked all over our room and bit us. The window, that was only fitted with chicken wire, was completely open to the thick bushes outside and we suffered at night from mosquito bites and the freezing cold air from Lake Victoria.

However, the atmosphere was friendly because the Tanzanian soldiers, under whose care we were, were kind and they gave us good food. Our main concern was our families. Not only did they not know our fate, they also did not know why we were arrested.

After about a week, an officer came to our room. He sat on a stool and in a casual, friendly manner, said that he wanted to know more about each of us. I pleaded with him to see to it that my two briefcases, taken upon my arrest, were returned to me. The following afternoon a soldier unlocked our door and ordered us out. We asked where we were going and he said we were going to a place with a better breeze. We were naturally apprehensive as we boarded a bus together with all the male

UPM members who were under arrest. A small, stern soldier ordered us not to turn our heads left, right or look behind. Whoever dared to disobey would get a bullet from the pistol in his hand, he threatened. We had no idea where we were going. Later, when we discussed the trip, Margaret Mbasasire likened the small, harsh soldier to Samuel Doe, who was the then military ruler of Liberia. Margaret, somehow, managed to make us laugh a lot, and that eased our anxiety somewhat.

The bus drove towards Kampala and entered the city through Entebbe Road. At the junction of the Kampala-Entebbe-Jinja roads, there was a traffic jam that was caused by a vehicle that had broken down. The soldiers on our bus panicked as they did not want us to be recognised by the public. However, before we left the spot, a friend who was passing by recognised me. She ran to my brother-in-law, Erisa Kironde, and told him that Rhoda Kalema was alive after all. As Psalm 138:7 states: "Though I walk in the midst of trouble, you preserve my life; you stretch out your hand against the anger of my foes, with your right hand you save me." (NIV)

Luzira

As the bus turned towards the main gate of the Luzira Maximum Security Prison, we were apprehensive. When we entered the prison, we underwent a cruel procedure. We were made to sit on the hot tarmac before we were counted. We each had to say out our number in Kiswahili, '*moja, mbili, tatu, nne, tano, sita…*' We each received a heavy slap on the cheek when we said our numbers. I awaited my turn and spoke out my number '*sita*' (six). The slap was so heavy that it left marks that lasted some time. Still reeling from the slaps, we were loaded onto a Land Rover that took us to the women's section of the prison. I was still in shock and feeling deeply humiliated when we were, once again, made to sit on the floor. The wardresses immediately assured us, with compassion, that we were now safe and that our names would be recorded in a government register so that we could be traced. Until then, there was no record of our arrests. That was when I realised that although I was alive, until that moment, I had been in a 'danger zone'. In that space where my family and the public did not know whether I was dead or alive, anyone could get rid of me, easily.

Suddenly, a wardress recognised me. "Are you not Mrs Kalema?" she asked. "Didn't your children go to school with my cousins?"

"I am the one," I replied. "Who are you?"

"I am Alice," she said. "I am the niece of Miss Esuka Mwase, your dormitory matron at Budo. She talks a lot about you."

This was like an unfolding fairy tale. Indeed, this was Alice Kisakye, the niece of my former house matron at King's College Budo! Her mother died giving birth to her and her mother's sister, Esuka Mwase, my house matron, brought her to live with her at the school when she was only two days old. We watched her grow and took turns bathing and babysitting her. I was very close to baby Alice; I even had a photo of her at two years old among my family photos. When she introduced herself, I recognised her; her face had not changed much.

The life that looked very dark a moment before, suddenly looked much brighter. The wardresses' daily routine took them into town and Alice offered to take a message to my sister Gladys Wambuzi and to get me some basic items like toothpaste, soap, sugar and a change of clothes, including a small towel. This was the first direct information my family got about me and they were very relieved. My sister hurriedly put together things that I might need and Alice brought them to me.

Just like it happened at the Katabi Barracks, the five of us were housed in a separate building from other prisoners. Because we were 'very dangerous', we were barely allowed outside. We were not given any work, not even cooking. All our meals were prepared using supplies brought in from the Katabi Barracks. We were 'prisoners of war' and were in the Luzira Prison only because there were no female quarters in the Katabi Barracks. We were fairly well accommodated, despite having to sleep on the floor without proper mattresses. We had a verandah which was enclosed by a high metal fence through which we could, at least, look outside. This made us feel like we had a little bit of freedom. I shared a cell and a woven sleeping mat (*ekirago*) on the floor with Sophie. Our entire group became friends. My fellow inmates developed a special respect for me, calling me 'mummy,' and they would not let me do my share of cleaning – either of the floor or the verandah.

The other four women in the group knew nothing about politics; their arrests were based on suspicions and false reports. I, at least, was 'guilty' of being a full participant in the creation of and campaigning for UPM. One morning, about two weeks later, a wardress called Jacinta was arrested and she joined us. She was suspected of being a UPM supporter. She told us that she was a DP member.

One day, Margaret Mbasasire told me that she had heard of me during the campaigns and had she known me, she would have come to warn me not to waste my time. She said, "I knew that any other political party was wasting its time campaigning against Obote's party." She continued, "I knew that even if Obote had only ten or twenty supporters, he would still have won the election and become President of Uganda again."

Margaret was a trader in men's suits and clothing at Apolo Hotel. She was well acquainted with many of the 'liberators'. She lost her shop to one of them. He framed her using some subversive story. Margaret remained in prison for a long time after my release. Remarkably, after all those years, in July 2019, I received a surprise call from Margaret and I visited her and we talked about our shared prison experience, among many other things.

In prison, I took the opportunity to tell my fellow inmates about God's love. I managed to get a Bible smuggled in through Alice. Although we were two Muslims, two Catholics and two Protestants, everyone admitted that they were encouraged by the words from the Bible. Among the stories we shared were those about the UPM and the things we dreamed for Uganda. We talked about the days of Amin and what we had all gone through. We all saw, clearly, how bad leaders can damage a country.

On Sundays, we got a chance to briefly get away from confinement. We were allowed to go for Sunday service with the 'less dangerous prisoners' that included people who were in remand and convicted criminals.

I developed back pain and when I was denied permission to go to the hospital, the prison doctor got me a mattress. This was noted by the security committee in Kampala that was dominated by high ranking army officers. A lady who was the committee secretary told her friend, Margaret Nasuna Kalema, who is my niece and who worked in the Ministry of Foreign

Affairs, "It is understood that Rhoda Kalema has the longest legs in prison and she gets special treatment." I was told about the comment after I left prison. The mattress, however, was not taken away.

* * *

When I was arrested, all my children were outside Uganda, except the youngest, Gladys Nalubowa, who was boarding at Kabale Preparatory School in western Uganda. William, who was in the USA, and Peter Martin, who was in London, decided to write to President Obote. Peter told the President that they did not want their mother to end up disappearing like their father. The two boys also decided that one of them would return to Kampala as soon as possible. I later learnt that Bishop Leslie Brown had also written to the president asking why I was arrested. He appealed to him to see to it that I was safe. When I visited the Browns in Cambridge in 1982, I saw a copy of the letter and the reply from the President. I believe that their great concern and boldness contributed significantly to my eventual release.

Peter's letter to President Obote was so daring that it alarmed the President's Permanent Secretary, Mr Zerubabel Bigirwenkya (this he told me later). Soon after, Peter hastily returned to Uganda leaving a good job in London, in order to tackle my imprisonment. He got in touch with my brother-in-law, Sam Wako Wambuzi who, because he was a former Chief Justice, had access to the president. Before long, the president agreed to meet my son and Justice Wambuzi.

On the morning of the 28th March 1981, as we were gazing as usual out of our barred windows like caged animals, we saw a top army officer, Colonel Sam Nanyumba, walking with a wardress towards our prison building. This was most unusual

Visit to Maama Erusa Nalubowa with nephews Philipo Mutebi, Dan Ndaula; children Peter Martin, Katerega and other relatives, December 1971

Our family home in Kiboga rebuilt

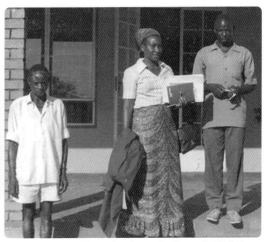

Matia Kasaija and Rhoda launching UPM in Kiboga town, November 1980

Petero Mpagazi, Rhoda and Abiasali Kalule in the 1980 campaigns

With Adonia Tiberondwa, Minister of Culture & Community Development, at World Refugee Day, at Oruchinga Valley in western Uganda, 1980

At home with all my six children, two daughters-in-law, (2ⁿᵈ left) Felleng and Juliet (3ʳᵈ right) and four grandchildren, December 1986

With grandchildren and Bex Woodsford L-R: Zalwango, Bex, Nabadda, Willie, Juko, Me and daughter, Gladys Nalubowa, 1996

Rhoda with Ignatius Musaazi and Mary Klopper, early 1990s

Bishop Leslie and Winifred Brown with Rhoda at their home
Cambridge, 1993

Rhoda with Pat Rhea, early 1990s

With Gladys Nalubowa after trekking Mountain Gorillas at Bwindi
Impenetrable Forest, 2000

Giving prizes after giving a talk at the Annual Rhoda Kalema Lecture, Kings College Budo, 2008

Family at Kiboga home, 2013. L-R Back: Lawrence, Rhoda, Nakibule, William, grandson Rwabukye, Nalubowa

In front: Grandchildren Ndhego, Samwiri, Tendo

Kabaka Ronald Mutebi planting tree at Kiboga home, July 2017

With Grandsons Rwabukye, Willie and Ntale, July 2017

With siblings. Seated L-R: Rhoda, Eseza, Eresi, Janet. Standing:
Robina, Semu, Gladys, John, December 2004

Maama Catherine and Taata Nelson Sebugwawo

and we were all scared stiff. What next? The wardress called: "Rhoda Kalema, come out."

I immediately changed into my long dress and bedroom slippers. Just as it was during my arrest, there was no explanation as to why I was leaving or where I was going. Imprisonment is an uncertain situation – one can only wait to see whether things move towards a better or worse end. The slight consolation I had was that I found Colonel Nanyumba to be a calm and reasonable person during my time at the NCC. He had been careful not to get embroiled in the political conflict – for or against UPM. His behaviour was that of a professional soldier the whole time.

I was first driven to the Prisons Commissioner's Office in Kampala before we left for the office of the Minister for Internal Affairs and finally, after a long wait, to State House, in Entebbe.

I was led into President Obote's office by Minister, Dr. John Luwuliza Kirunda. I must mention that Kirunda looked very uncomfortable at seeing me in such a state. My husband was very fond of him when he was a student at Makerere and when he passed his medical degree in 1967, he walked to our house on Nakasero Hill Road to give us the good news. William had congratulated him with a gift of 500 shillings – quite a bit of money at the time, and Kirunda never forgot that kind gesture.

In President Obote's office, I found Justice Wambuzi and my son Peter Martin who wept when he saw me. I had no idea that he was back in Kampala. Without hesitation, President Obote announced that Justice Wambuzi and my son were there to take me home, but Justice Wambuzi had to guarantee 'my behaviour' if I was to be released. He then turned to me.

"You are free to do whatever you want. I do not stop you from carrying on with your subversive activities."

I looked intently at the president as he addressed me and as soon as I thought he was done speaking, I responded. "Your Excellency, I am glad that I am released from prison," I said. "However, I would like to clarify one thing. From what you said, you have set me free and you do not stop me from carrying out subversive activities. I am afraid I did not understand what you meant by that. I never participated in any subversive activities. I was arrested from my home." By the time I finished my response, Justice Wambuzi – as he later told me – almost fainted. That, he said, was because he wondered, "What if Obote orders her back in prison for daring to challenge him?"

President Obote then informed me that I was to hand my passport to the Ministry of Internal Affairs or to the Criminal Investigations Department (CID). I told him that I had two passports, a regular one and a diplomatic one having been a government minister up to the time elections were held in December 1980. He declared that in his whole life, he had never known anyone who voluntarily admitted to having two passports so they could hand them in. He then ordered three rolls of women's fabric for me from the State House store. I did not need them, but I thanked him all the same and took them. I gave them to people in Kiboga. I was finally free after seven weeks in detention.

* * *

I started reporting to the CID as I had been ordered to, but with decreasing frequency; once a week for over six months, then once a fortnight and finally once a month for a year. My two briefcases, which I had constantly clamoured for, were eventually brought to my home. However, some of my documents including a land title deed and the document on the Moshi Conference, were missing.

Many people visited me to offer their sympathies over my ordeal – despite the prevailing dangerous and unpredictable political atmosphere. That year, my sister, Janet paid me regular visits as I recovered; her visits reduced my loneliness and anxiety. In 1982, I needed to travel to the UK and the USA and sought permission from President Obote. He granted the request, but I knew I was being monitored. While in Britain, I restrained myself from visiting Professor Yusuf Lule at his London home for fear of repercussions upon my return. I was aware, of course, that the UPC had played a part in his removal in 1979, so that they could regain power. He had been my beloved teacher at King's College Budo and Hannah, his wife, was my wonderful girls' prefect at the same school. We later became great family friends but, given the circumstances, I had to be content with speaking to them on phone. I state all this to show how haphazard political life can be and the apprehension one lives with when a country is destabilised. This experience haunted me for a long time as Yusuf Lule died in London in 1985 without me ever meeting him again.

Peter did not go back to his job in the UK. Our family friend, James Mulwana offered him free office space on Kampala Road where he established his Estate Management company, Kalema-Kayondo & Co., which he operated for twelve years.

My Spiritual Renewal

My arrest and subsequent incarceration was a major spiritual test for me. Coupled with other earlier weighty experiences, they showed me that though I may be surrounded by threats, the assurance of God's deliverance was calming and could give me peace. I drew inspiration from Psalm 91:14-16 (NIV), which states, "Because he loves me," says the Lord, "I will rescue him; I will protect him, for he acknowledges my name. He will call upon me, and I will answer him; I will be with him in trouble, I will deliver him and honour him. With long life, I will satisfy him and show him my salvation."

Soon after my release from prison, a friend and fellow Christian, Eseri, came to visit me and she read Psalm 119:71 (NIV) with me. It revealed the profit of God's chastisement. "It was good for me to be afflicted so that I might learn your decrees." It was easy for me to see this in my life. I could have been killed on the night I was taken from my house. It is at that point that God brought a fresh hunger into my heart and challenged me on my insufficient spiritual life.

When my last two daughters were young, I had served as a Sunday School teacher, a church warden, a member of the church council and a reader of lessons in church. I even arranged altar flowers at All Saints Cathedral.

It dawned on me that I had lost the joy and assurance of the full spiritual life that I had received in July 1949. Re-reading through old copies of the monthly *Guideposts* magazines, I found many testimonies on how God worked in people's lives and I was inspired anew. Articles on 'His Mysterious Ways' and 'This Thing Called Prayer' also made an impression. I continued seeking to regain that comfortable place with my God whom I had once loved passionately.

On 11th December, 1983, my great friend and sister in the Lord, Eseza Kalimuzo and I were invited by her daughter, Rose, to a School of Ministry Convention at King's College Budo. Although we were there for only one day, the convention provided what I was looking for. Travelling back home, I heard a fresh voice in my heart – the Lord challenging me with words from John 10:10 (RSV) that declare: "The thief comes only to steal and kill and destroy; I came that they may have life, and have it abundantly." I examined my life and realised that I did not have abundant life, yet the Son of God came that I may have nothing less than abundant life.

I decided to start afresh and focus on God and I repented about my lukewarm attitude while absorbed in political activities, and the many sins I had glossed over. I consider 11ᵗʰ December 1983, my second spiritual rebirth.

Arrest Again: The Truth is Out

I had hardly regained my peace when another arrest was carried out in February 1983, after I visited my daughter Betty in Nairobi. I had by then been 'discharged' by the CID and I no longer had to report to their offices. On the day of departure, when I was at Entebbe Airport, Vice President Paulo Muwanga found me sitting in the VIP lounge.

"Where are you going?" he asked.

"I am travelling to Nairobi to visit my children," I replied.

"Ooh!" he said and went to another VIP lounge upstairs. Before long, a young man came and asked me to vacate the VIP lounge because I was not a VIP. Of course, I obliged and went to the waiting area where all the seats were taken. I had a difficult wait until we boarded the place. Having complied with the authority's directive, I thought that was the end of the story. However, it seems that as soon as I left Entebbe, Vice President Muwanga alerted the Immigration Department to watch out for me on my return.

On the return flight from Nairobi three days later, I sat next to a UPM comrade, James Musinguzi and he promised to give me a lift home from Entebbe Airport. At the immigration desk, an officer took my passport, read my name and asked me to follow a police officer. It was about eight o'clock in the morning. I was taken to the police officers' room and made to wait. The unhappy police officers kept apologising, saying that they were still contacting Kampala for orders. I was finally made to write a statement. I had returned intending to get home in time to travel to the funeral of a good family friend, Phan Ntende, in Busoga. I realised that I was not going to make it after all.

Musinguzi had been behind me at the immigration desk and saw me being whisked away. He also noticed that I had not reappeared. He waited for some time before setting off for Kampala. He went to my son Peter's office and told him what had happened. After waiting for me for a while, my son drove to Entebbe Airport.

Peter Martin had very little time for what he considered 'nonsense' and he was extremely angry about the unnecessary persecution of his mother. He arrived at the airport at about two o'clock in the afternoon and straight away engaged the police officers, showing them his business card. In my statement, I had mentioned his name, where he worked and his telephone number and his card held the same information.

To the police, this was a good sign and a chance to get out of what they considered an extremely embarrassing situation. They had no answer to my son's incessant questions about why they held me for over six hours. Despite the pressure they were receiving from 'Kampala', they let him take me home. They seemed apologetic about what had happened. However, the airport police directed that I report to the Central Police Station in Kampala as soon as possible. I did, the following day.

On my way to the Central Police Station, I found Sarah Mulwana at Peter's office premises waiting for me. She offered to accompany me, fearing that I might not return from my encounter with the police. When I reported to the police station, I realised that the police had been informed that my name was on the list of guerrillas who were with Museveni in the bush. They had been told that "Rhoda Kalema has a battalion that she commands in Singo." An officer spent about an hour trying to find my name on his five-page long list as he asked over and over again, "What is your name? I cannot see it here." He eventually gave up. Nevertheless, I had to continue reporting to the station for a few weeks. I was comforted that Sarah was with me throughout as I was questioned.

Later, I learnt from reliable sources that it was Vice President Paulo Muwanga's orders, not President Obote's, that led to my being detained in February 1981 and in February 1983. What could have been the cause of such deep bitterness against me? I reflected on his animosity and I could only come to one conclusion.

Paulo Muwanga's antipathy towards me could be traced back to August and September 1979, when a period of great insecurity erupted in Kampala. Several doctors were murdered in their homes at night, including doctors from the Kampala City Council Health Centre, Dr Bagenda and Dr Kamulegeya (who was killed with his wife) and dentist Dr Jack Barlow. I remember calling Paulo Muwanga first thing in the morning to find out whether he knew about the shocking murder of Dr Jack Barlow. Around the same time, Enoch Olinga, a leader of the Bahai faith, and four members of his family, were also murdered at his home in Kampala. It was reported that a suspect in the murders of Olinga's family, Semakula, had been arrested and remanded at Luzira Maximum Security Prison. However, a few days later, news broke out that he had escaped and could not be traced. The nation was outraged. In the NCC, Muwanga, as the Minister for Internal Affairs, was asked to explain Semakula's escape.

The following day, Muwanga responded. He explained that the suspect had been allowed to eat his food outside his cell and that was how he had escaped. On the floor of parliament, I asked, "How could a suspect in a maximum security prison have been allowed to have his meals outside his cell, according to the Minister's explanation? Was it not clear that such a situation would give the suspect a chance to escape?" I was later told by a fellow member of the NCC that I had been very tough on the minister. Perhaps he never expected such a direct challenge. I later came to know that Muwanga told a confidant, "Rhoda believes that I killed the doctors." I think that this might have been the reason behind his actions and hostility when he became vice president in 1981.

These experiences have all given me a deep understanding of what my husband had once described to me as "the haphazard nature of politics." I was never bitter towards Paulo Muwanga as a person; after all, his behaviour was part of the chaotic and haphazard nature of our politics. Whatever happened to me regarding my arrests was God's plan for my life. As one poet[23] said in a poem that I love:

---

23 The poem is attributed to both Benjamin Malachi Franklin (1882-1965) and Grant Colfax Tullar (1869-1950)

My life is but a weaving
Between the Lord and me,
I cannot choose the colours
He worketh steadily

Oft' times He weaveth sorrow
And I, in foolish pride
Forget He sees the upper
And I the underside.

Not 'til the loom is silent
and the shuttles cease to fly,
shall God unroll the canvas
and explain the reason why.

The dark threads are as needful
in the weaver's skilful hand
As the threads of gold and silver
In the pattern he has planned.

He knows, He loves, He cares,
Nothing this truth can dim
He gives the very best to those
Who leave the choice to Him.

Chapter 15

A Deeper Faith, Family Bereavement

Even in the midst of my country's uncertain political future, I continued to grow spiritually. Among those who had a tremendous influence on my spiritual life around then were Pat Rhea and her husband, Dr Al Rhea. The couple first came to Uganda in 1982 as staff members of the Campus Crusade for Christ International. They first worked in Hoima, in western Uganda, where Al was a director of preventive health programmes and afterwards, they stayed on and worked with the LIFE Ministry (Lay Involvement for Evangelism) who were partners of the Campus Crusade.

I first interacted closely with the Rheas when I was invited by the LIFE Ministry to attend EXPLO'85, a worldwide convention that was organised by the Campus Crusade at Makerere University. I was very inspired by the Campus Crusade's work around the world. One day, at the end of the morning session, Pat invited a few women outside. We sat on the grass as she told us about a lady named Verna Birkey who was the head of the Enriched Living Ministry in the United States, and that she was scheduled to visit Kenya in 1987. She explained that the Enriched Living Ministry encouraged spiritual enrichment through individual Bible study, as well as Bible study groups. Pat informed us that she wanted her to visit Uganda during that tour. At that gathering, we formed a women's group that later became the Kampala International Christian Women Association (KICWA) and I was a member of the KICWA organising committee.

We mobilised many Christian women – mostly around Kampala – for the first Enriched Living Seminar that was officiated by Verna Birkey, in May 1987. At the two-day seminar during which I felt very blessed, Pat and I became close. Unknown to me, the experience was preparing my spirit for the great shocks that would be caused by family tragedies.

Pat Rhea further mobilised most of the women who had attended the Enriched Living Women's Seminar into a Bible study group that met in her house. Among the group leaders were Geraldine Kawuma, the wife of Misaeri Kawuma, the Bishop of Namirembe; Grace Kirya, and Sara Kibowa. The Rheas moved house a lot, but wherever they lived, we had the Bible studies that contributed to my loving and believing in the scriptures more deeply.

A New Government in Uganda

President Obote was overthrown by his army commanders, Brigadier Bazilio Olara Okello and General Tito Okello in July 1985. The new leaders invited all the groups to participate in a broad-based government. Museveni, who had occupied Tooro in Western Uganda, refused to join in and he was invited to the Nairobi Peace Talks. In spite of the talks, fighting continued and on 26th January 1986 Kampala fell. Museveni was sworn in as President on 29th January 1986.

With a new government in place, it looked like the political turmoil in Uganda had come to an end. The government formulated a programme of national reconstruction, which, among other things, would re-institute democracy, ensure security for all the people and their property, revive the economy and restore social services. Once again, Ugandans could afford to be optimistic.

In fact, in December of that year, my son William visited Uganda for the first time since 1971. The visit made it possible for the family to carry out an important cultural ceremony that saw him installed as his father's heir. He had a good career with Du Pont and in 1987, he was promoted to the position of executive assistant at the corporate headquarters in Wilmington, Delaware. He was being prepared for a senior position in research and development. However, that soon changed.

Death of Betty

Just as we were settling in with the new government, a second family tragedy, the death of our daughter, Betty, 36, occurred.

On the morning of 22nd August 1987, Betty brought her children to me for the weekend, as she sometimes did. That night, as she drove home from a Shell office gathering, Betty died in a car accident. The circumstances surrounding the accident were later thought to be extremely suspicious and pointed at foul play. It is neither easy, nor fair, for me to narrate the details of the circumstances of her death in this book. The experience was extremely shocking, bewildering and painful. My whole family and I were terribly shaken.

As the eldest child, Betty was very special to us. She was motherly and wise and she often gave me advice about her younger siblings, about which, I must admit, she was often right. She was very practical and she taught herself how to bake and sew. She even made her bridal gown and together with her great friend, Emma Negesa Lugujjo, she made her bridesmaids' dresses. Betty was also very warm, friendly and generous. Many years later, she was still warmly remembered by her many friends and schoolmates who kept in touch with us. Their friendship brings us great consolation and rekindles wonderful memories of my beloved daughter.

Death of Katerega

Almost nine months after Betty's death, a third tragedy occurred. On 28th May 1988, our fourth-born, Apolo Katerega died in Ward 16 at Mulago Hospital where he had been readmitted for observation. He never recovered completely from his mental illness.

After a successful first year at the London School of Economics (LSE), where he enrolled in 1979, he gradually sunk into a depression. It was a while before my family and I realised the extent of his problem. From 1981, he experienced mental health challenges and was in and out of hospitals in England and Uganda. Throughout his school life at Kitante Primary School and Budo, Apolo had many friends. Among his best friends, till the end of his life, was Joe Oloka-Onyango, a prominent lawyer and academician.

The deaths of my two children in quick succession were emotionally draining. I received a lot of support from family and friends and one great source of solace was Pat Rhea who remained close by my side. She gifted me a small booklet titled *God's Promises,* which contained a number of significant

Psalms. For Betty's funeral service, I chose Psalm 139 (NIV) from *God's Promises* for the reading. Verse 1 reads:

O LORD, you have searched me and you know me.

You know when I sit down and when I rise,

You perceive my thoughts from a far.

Verse 7 states:

Where can I go from your Spirit?

Where can I flee from your presence?

I continued to learn that God has complete control over our lives and His faithfulness endures.

Writing My Spiritual Journey

In October 1988, I honoured my son William's invitation to visit them in the United States of America. He was hoping that the change of scene would help me diffuse the overwhelming sadness within me. When I arrived in Wilmington, I was dispirited and my mind was blank. I could hardly sleep or eat, despite the loving care I received from my son and my daughter-in-law, Felleng, and the pleasure of being with my lovely eight-month old grandson, William 'Willie' Emmanuel Ndaula. In an effort to get me back to 'normal', my son took away the sleeping tablets that had been prescribed by my doctor in Uganda.

One day, after three weeks, I 'came around' and 'rediscovered' myself. I felt normal and I even started to sleep well. William was right about the sleeping tablets. I hardly prayed when I was on them. Without them, I was able to pray and God faithfully comforted me and I gradually accepted my loss. In His plan, He said to me, "It is time for you to write down what you have gone through in your life, with me beside you." Since Felleng had a typewriter and I still could type, I found myself, without a draft, typing all that God brought to my mind about my journey in His hands. I called the story, 'My Spiritual Journey'. That was in 1988 and I did not imagine that I would be alive thirty three years later.

God took me back to the early days of my life. What I wrote then would have given my children and friends a brief history about my life – my conversion one afternoon in July 1949, at Mengo Palace when I 'got saved', my encounter with the *Abalokole,* my life as a young mother and my tribulations after the death of my husband.

Looking back on those forty years of my spiritual journey, I realised that Christ and His salvation message to me and all humankind has never changed. The strength of my faith, had, however, varied from time to time, particularly when my family experienced bereavement. There were times when I would ask God, "God, where were you when this happened?"

Now, years later, I realise that God has His divine way of directing our paths to reach Him. As Psalm 31:15 (NIV) states, "My times are in your hands…"

During my stay in Wilmington, Pat and Al were on holiday in Atlanta, Georgia, and Pat invited me to their home. Al was away in the Philippines conducting a training conference but I got to meet their daughter Nancy, their son Alfred, his wife Loren and their children. The memorable five days I spent with her family deepened our friendship. Pat also arranged for me to attend the World Missions Conference led by Dr Charles Stanley, the former President of the Southern Baptist Convention and the author of *In Touch Ministries* – a devotional magazine. During the conference at the First

Baptist Church in Atlanta, Pat spoke about her mission in Uganda and she gave me a few minutes of her time to address the participants.

In August 1989, she forwarded my name to the Nairobi International Christian Women's Association (NICWA) so that I could share my life experience that was a testimony of God's power and faithfulness at the association's luncheon. I was anxious and shaky at the beginning of my talk but Pat, who was ever supportive, encouraged me. Kenyan women responded warmly to my message and I received touching letters from them after I returned home.

Meanwhile, KICWA continued the work that was started by Verna Birkey and the Enriched Living Ministry. We held the first Biblical Seminar in September 1989, and the second in 1991 at the Baptist Church in Nakulabye, Kampala. These seminars influenced my life and the lives of the women who gave testimonies that illustrated how they had experienced divine growth in their spiritual lives. Sharing the Gospel through Bible study was a new experience for most of us. The Enriched Living Ministry and KICWA's work empowered us to reach out to other women so that they could relate to Jesus through Bible study. As Selywn Hughes stated in the *Every Day With Jesus (EDWJ)* edition of 11th December 2016, "… the better we know the Bible, the better we will know God."

Pat also introduced me to Mr and Mrs Johnson, who were members of the Campus Crusade International. The Johnsons held Bible study classes for young children and on some evenings, I would drive my four grandchildren, Zalwango, Nabadda, Juko, and Ntale to their house for classes.

In 1995, the Rheas left Uganda and returned to the USA where they continued working with the Campus Crusade for Christ International. After ten years working with Pat, saying goodbye was hard, but speaking about their devoted work and devotion to KICWA at their farewell party was easy. We kept in touch and they sent me regular communiques and prayer requests for the work at the executive ministries. They also sent me books, including, *The Joy of Spirit-filled Living* by Dr Bill Bright and the *Quiet Moment with Bill Bright,* a collection of 120 daily readings. Sadly, Pat passed away on 28th December 2019, aged 85, in Atlanta.

Chapter 16

National Resistance Council and Constituent Assembly

As stated earlier, my home in Kiboga is in the 'Luwero Triangle' area where Museveni waged his guerrilla war from February 1981 to January 1986. I did not visit Kiboga at all during those five years. When I eventually visited in early February 1986, I was struck by the devastation. The destruction and damage along the main road, was especially depressing.

During the war, NRM created Resistance Councils (RCs) which were self-government structures at the local level. These were its political and logistical support systems, in the areas that had been captured by NRM. After redefining the councils through a series of legal instruments, a five-tiered system of councils known as RCs I-V, was created at the district level and established all over the country after 1986. The district council formulated development plans, approved annual estimates and formulated by-laws. There was commitment at each RC level to ensure that women and young people were represented.

I was elected chairperson of the Resistance Council I (RCI) in my area, the lowest council level of a village or ward (in towns and cities) in which all residents were members. The local councils were empowered with functions, including identifying local problems, making recommendations, and implementing solutions. Thereafter, the elected committees formed into electoral colleges that elected other councils. I was also elected a member of the RCII in Kiboga Town in December 1988.

Joining the National Resistance Council and Government

In January 1989, concerned about Kiboga, I was compelled to make an appointment and meet Hon. Amanya Mushega, the Minister for Local Government. He had been Betty and William's friend at King's College Budo. Trusting in the mutual spirit of UPM, I wished to discuss the reconstruction and development of social services, schools and health centres in the Kiboga sub-district.

"Well, if you are so concerned about Kiboga," Mushega said to me, "you should offer to stand as a member of the National Resistance Council and you can express your concerns officially and with authority in parliament. We are holding elections at the end of February."

It was then that I learnt that the government was planning to expand the NRC.

From 1986 to 1996, the NRC functioned as the legislature and was known as the Fifth Parliament. At the time, it consisted of ninety-eight nominated members that included former NRA/NRM combatants, and some technocrats and professionals who were appointed to serve as ministers in their fields of expertise. Some of the professionals were: Victoria Sekitoleko, who became Minister for Agriculture; Joyce Rovincer Mpanga, the Minister for Education; and Architect

Mutebi Mulwanira, who was appointed Minister for Housing and Urban Development. The 1986 NRC government held office until February 1989 when the decision was made to expand it.

The representatives joined the 'historical' members who came together in the bush during the resistance war. The NRC therefore, comprised of: ten representatives of the NRA, one representative elected by the district councils in each of the thirty-eighty districts, five youth representatives, three workers' representatives, twenty presidential nominees, one representative from each division of the City of Kampala, a representative from each municipality; Jinja got two, though, because it was larger.

The election method was kept simple as there was no time to implement the regular adult suffrage. Moreover, there was no constitution or electoral law in place as yet. The elections were to be carried out by the electoral colleges of RCIII and RCV in each county and voters were required to line up behind the candidate of their choice – in broad daylight!

Voting day was scheduled for 25th February 1989.

Although I had already been elected RCI chairperson of Kiboga town, I hesitated in running for elections lest I end up in more political trouble, which I thought would not be fair to my children. However, I also carefully considered Amanya Mushega's advice.

I shall always remember 10th February 1989, when Mary Klopper and I travelled to Kiboga for a visit to my country home. She was visiting Uganda with her husband, Professor Arnold Klopper, who was an external examiner at Makerere University's Medical School. This memorable visit with Mary turned out to have political implications.

We travelled in my small pick-up and she did not seem to mind the bumpy and dusty road. Mary was only interested in all the political and education-related activities that I was involved in. We visited the primary school that my husband, William, attended in the early 1930s and she donated some money for a small radio, "so that the children may access more information and learn better."

The next day, we paid the Assistant District Administrator (ADA), Sula Sserunjogi, a courtesy call in his office. He was a former NRA guerrilla fighter so before long, the visit turned into a political discussion. Both Mary and the ADA raised the issue of my vying for the NRC seat and they expressed very strong sentiments about why I should participate in the forthcoming elections. I listened to them and, finally, I was persuaded.

That was how I ended up as a candidate for Kiboga County in the February 1989 elections where I ran against Daniel Kiwalabye Musoke. On polling day, 321 people lined up behind me while Kiwalabye had 105 people behind him. Having won 75 per cent of the vote, I became the Kiboga member of the NRC.

The expanded NRC was sworn in on 6th April 1989. The first debate took place on 11th April at the Parliament Building in Kampala with the Chairman of the NRC, Haji Musa Kigongo, as Speaker. Although the initial plan was that national elections would be held again after four years, it was later realised that this was not going to be practical or possible and the period was extended to seven years. This was because all the basic state institutions – the judiciary, the police, army, civil service and social services needed to be rebuilt.

On 20th April, 1989, I was appointed Deputy Minister for Public Service and Cabinet Affairs. I viewed my appointment, that would involve the rebuilding of a broken public service, as a great challenge. The country needed public servants with integrity, people who would be capable of working hard – in the spirit of the pre-independence days and the first eight years of independence. All the same, it was great experience managing the public service that I had served thirty years earlier.

I was primarily tasked with reviewing the roles of all civil servants and eliminating 'ghost workers', a term that referred to 'non-existent workers' who were added to the payroll by dishonest officials who then drew the salaries, allowances and other benefits, under those names. Inflated lists of workers were a big drain on the country's resources and the ministry sent teams to all the government departments around the country to verify the existence of all the workers. At the time, I believed that it was possible to resolve the problem within a very short time and this was important because the reform of the civil service was one of the conditions given for Uganda to access assistance from the International Monetary Fund (IMF). We did not succeed in resolving the problem and for a long time afterwards, 'ghost workers' continued to feature on the government's payroll.

I also oversaw the opening and closing of workshops and seminars at the Uganda Management Training Institute. However, I cannot say that I enjoyed that task much. That was because the role of the Deputy Minister could be frustrating at times as one could not always speak one's mind. At most events, I read speeches that were written by the permanent secretary – speeches that I considered to be 'dry'. However, by the time I left the ministry, I was writing and reading my own speeches.

The World Bank advised the government to bring down the expenditure of the public service by reducing the number of ministers and other public officials and in June 1991, I was retired.

One remarkable carry-away from my service was Simon Kiiza, a driver from Hoima, who decided to leave the ministry and continue working for me although he knew that I could not afford to pay him a big salary. Simon, who was like a son to me, stayed with me until he met his untimely death in May, 1993. His mother Rosemary and brothers are still my friends.

NRC Constituency Work

After I retired from the ministerial position, since I was still a member of the NRC, I devoted most of my time to the development of the Kiboga Sub-District. If asked about my political life during the period 1989 to 1996, I would say that this was the period that I enjoyed the most and I still remember the time with a lot of pleasure.

I found it difficult to handle 'politics' as a separate entity from the people's welfare – for what is politics if it is not connected to the people's good? I did not consider people to be mere 'votes' that would keep me in the NRC; they were citizens I needed to stay close to, serve and enlighten, so that they could achieve good health, economic independence and lead dignified lives. I wanted the people to feel and understand that they had a stake in their country because it belonged to them. I valued the time I spent with the people, appreciating their individual worth and their hunger for development.

I used the NRC platform to achieve whatever I could access for Kiboga, in particular, opportunities for education and health services. I also used the platform to lobby for the improvement of the Kampala-Hoima Road that passes through Kiboga. After many years, a smooth tarmac road would finally be constructed.

The poor quality of government services was a constant concern for me. One day, I mentioned to the NRC that a doctor had demanded money from three expectant mothers (who later died) 'to fuel' the Kiboga Hospital generator. Yet the Ministry of Health sent money every month to ensure that the maternity, theatre and children's wards remained connected in case of power failure. The Medical Council summoned the doctor and he was immediately transferred out of Kiboga.

I was in the NRC until April 1996 when I decided to retire, one month before the national elections of 9th May 1996. The new constitution had already been effected on 8th October 1995 and its promulgation was the result of a process that had begun way back in 1988 and culminated in its enactment by the Constituent Assembly (CA).

Constituent Assembly (May 1994 - October 1995)

With all the political upheavals that took place between the end of Amin's regime and 1986, the atmosphere was not conducive for the writing of a new constitution. When the NRM government took over the leadership, many of Amin's decrees were still in place. A new constitution was one of the basic objectives that the NRM set for rebuilding the country.

On 21st December 1988, the NRC voted to establish a commission that would commence the process of formulating a new constitution and the Uganda Constitutional Commission was formally inaugurated on 24th March 1989. It consisted of twenty-one members – mostly lawyers and civil servants – with Justice Benjamin Odoki as its chairman. It was known as the

Odoki Commission. As part of its mandate, the commissioners travelled around the country collecting people's views on what their expectations were regarding the new constitution.

Members of the public responded with great enthusiasm. I attended the sessions in Kiboga and one response to the question, "What kind of president do you want?" caught my attention. The respondent, an elderly man, had walked twelve miles to get to the session. Holding onto his three foolscaps that had his answers written in Luganda, he replied, "We do not want '*nakyemalira*' (a dictator) like Saddam Hussein." This made Hajj Aziz Kasujja, the Chairman of the Electoral Commission, break into hearty laughter. "Mrs Kalema, you have men in this area," he told me. This was in a remote part of the Kiboga area where one did not expect the local residents to be aware of international politics. I mention this incident because to me, it was evidence that citizens were really concerned about their country's leadership.

I believe that Ugandans took a keen interest in the exercise because they had experienced bad leadership for a long time and yearned for good governance. Using the information that was gathered, questionnaires were prepared and sent around the country in 1992.

The Commission received feedback from more than 25,000 respondents and the final report, including a draft constitution, was presented in December 1992. The Commission recommended that a Constituent Assembly, elected by the people – that would also include the representatives of a few interest groups – be constituted to give the proposed constitution greater legitimacy. It was also decided that the Assembly would debate each chapter of the draft constitution.

The government accepted the proposal and the Constituent Assembly Bill was drafted, debated and passed by the NRC. This paved the way for the nomination and election of candidates from the various constituencies. Some candidates were already members of the NRC while others were not.

I have had considerable interest in the nation's constitution since 1960. I still have, in my possession, copies of the 1962, 1966, 1967, and 1995 constitutions. I was, therefore, very interested in representing my district in the writing of the nations new constitution.

The ground for Uganda's Independence Constitution was laid by the Wild Committee of 1959, set up by J. Vernon Wild, on self-government for Uganda, and the Munster Commission of 1961, on the best form of government for an independent Uganda. Reports of the two panels formed the basis for the 1962 constitutional discussions that were finalised at two London conferences. The first at Lancaster House in 1961, and the second at Marlborough House in 1962. Although ordinary Ugandans were not involved in the making of the Constitution, the Wild Committee and the Munster Commission deliberations were attended by delegates from the various kingdoms, regions and political parties. The 1962 Constitution was suspended in February 1966 and later in April the 1966 Constitution was introduced without notice, placed in parliamentary pigeonholes already completed. People still refer to it as 'the pigeonhole constitution'. The 1967 Constitution, which formally abolished the kingdoms and chieftaincy of Busoga, was debated by a constituent assembly made up of parliamentarians. The importance of broad participation in the making of the new constitution could not be overemphasised. Ugandans regarded it as special since they were contributing to its making.

By that time, Kiboga District had two constituencies – Kiboga East and Kiboga West. In each district, a position was reserved for a woman representative. While the elections to the NCC and the NRC had been simple and did not attract many candidates, the CA elections proved to be very popular. They were heavily contested due to increased awareness among citizens. I vied in the Kiboga East constituency against eight men. I held individual and joint campaign meetings with my competitors. The CA seat campaign provided a great opportunity for me to reach many people, educate them and at the same time, consult them on the contents of the Draft Constitution.

To many, the constitution was making sense for the first time. I remember how once, at a rally, when I asked the crowd what they thought about Ugandans using one language, a number of them said that it was necessary. They argued, "If even the cocks and chickens have a 'chicken *olukoko*' (ko-ko-ko), why not us, the people of one country?" A lady journalist who accompanied me recorded all the comments and they were published in the *Ngabo* newspaper.

Meeting people and hearing their views gave me and, I believe, the other CA delegates, the understanding that the citizens had faith in and supported the exercise. Furthermore, involving the people made me understand that a constitution was not just a legal document, it was a political contract. It had the people's political wishes on how they should or should not be governed. In it, they executed their responsibility towards the creation of lasting peace and stability in the country and expressed ideals that were going to be passed on to future generations. Significantly, the first article of the constitution states: "All power belongs to the people".

With this in mind, on 29th April 1994, I wrote a letter to the Kiboga East Sub-Counties and parishes asking for their views. Attached was a Luganda translation of the CA issues that were being discussed. After the CA was opened a month later, in May 1994, I visited the people and it was clear that they understood what was going on.

As I campaigned, I told the people about the United States of America Constitution which, at the time, was about 200 years old. I had the privilege of visiting the room where the Constitution was concluded in 1787, in Philadelphia, Pennsylvania, when I visited my family in Delaware, in 1988.

Remembering what I learnt during that visit was a driving force for me. I assured the people that our new constitution was going to last as long as the American one, because our country had experienced great suffering as is reflected in the preamble in the Uganda Constitution.

The CA elections were held in May 1994 and I won the Kiboga East seat. Soon after, elected delegates were sworn in and work began under the Chairmanship of Hon. James Wapakhabulo and Vice Chairperson, Professor Victoria Mwaka. The CA, made up of 284 delegates, sat at the International Conference Centre in Kampala and at the first meeting, each delegate was given half an hour to introduce their general views as they wished them debated. All the speeches were recorded and I still have my printed speech delivered on 21st July 1994. Below is an excerpt.

> Madam Chairperson and Honourable Delegates,
> I have come with an open mind on behalf of my
> people, determined to work out a constitution
> together with all of you that will establish

reconciliation, democracy, peace, unity and prosperity for everyone in our country and then we shall create a new Uganda nation... I was among those people who had so much hope in the liberation that came with the liberators in April 1979 after the fall of Amin. There were many doctors and professors. As a matter of fact, excited people used to ask, Sir, you are professor who? Which meant that the liberators were all qualified and educated people. I also offered myself for the National Consultative Council, because I wanted to attempt to rebuild the country, but peace eluded us again...I know that everyone here is clear about the extreme and unprecedented violation of human rights that has happened in our motherland. I am sure that is why we are all here to attempt to give Ugandans a good chance to govern themselves sensibly for generations to come...

I also appealed to the delegates to consider seriously and implement the recommendations of the commission's report on marriage, divorce, and the status of women.

Specialised discussions were held by six committees and each had two or three chapters to work on. I was in Committee Number Five that dealt with 'political systems'. It was chaired by Hon. Eriya Kategaya. We discussed and reviewed political parties and the 'movement' system that was first introduced in 1980 through the UPM and was the foundation of the 1986 NRM government. Our committee's main consideration was the identification of the system that was most suitable for promoting and sustaining unity and democracy. The committee recommended that political parties be kept out and the 'movement system' be allowed to continue for ten years to enable it to consolidate the country's unity first.

My personal and sincere belief at the time was that after that, the citizens would be ready to select a political system of their choice when people were more united as a nation. However, I regretted my stand later when I realised that political parties should have been introduced sooner for the role they play in widening political space. I mention this because I believe that broad political participation is necessary if a country is to sustain its unity, democracy and social justice.

The new constitution was promulgated on 8th October 1995, at the International Conference Centre and the event preceded the nation's 33rd independence anniversary by a day. It was received enthusiastically and many smaller copies were printed in the English language. I bought copies and handed one to each of the five sub-counties in my constituency.

It was intended that the constitution would be translated into local languages around the same time. Unfortunately, more than a quarter of a century later, the Constitution's Chapter One, Article 4, that required that the constitution be translated into local languages, has not been implemented. The Article clearly states, "The State shall promote public awareness of this constitution by translating it into Ugandan languages and disseminating it as widely as possible; and providing for the teaching of the constitution in all educational institutions and armed forces training institutions and regularly, transmitting and publishing programmes through the media generally."

I wrote two articles about this issue and they were published in the *New Vision* newspaper in 2004 and later in 2009. I even raised the matter with the Speaker of the Parliament and his deputy. My efforts did not yield the desired result; so I can only pray that it happens in my lifetime.

William's Return to Uganda

With the death of Betty in 1987, followed by Katerega's in 1988, William increasingly felt the need to return home and take up his family responsibilities. So, despite his successful career in the United States, in November 1991, he took leave of absence from Du Pont and moved to Uganda. From the start, he worked closely with James Mulwana, who was the Chairman of the Uganda Manufacturers Association (UMA) and a pillar of the indigenous private sector in Uganda. William's first job in Uganda was that of chief executive of the budding UMA consultancy service, the Uganda Manufacturers Association Consultancy and Information Services (UMACIS).

Although Du Pont took an exceptional step and extended his leave of absence for a second year, he took early retirement in October 1993. A major factor that influenced his decision was another family bereavement, the sudden death of his younger brother, Peter Martin Kayondo, in August 1993.

At the beginning of January 1981, Peter Martin came home and married Juliet Semambo, a former schoolmate at King's College Budo. He had already qualified as a Chartered Surveyor in the United Kingdom and after the wedding, the couple returned to London.

When I was imprisoned, he decided to return home and rescue me. Peter stayed on and set up Kalema Kayondo Company, a surveyors, valuers and estate agent consulting company. Although he was the sole partner, he had members of staff who he trained on the job. He was very professional and before long, he gained the confidence of government agencies, banks and embassies and his company was registered in the Royal Institute of Chartered Surveyors 1983 Yearbook, in the UK.

Peter Martin died after only three days of illness and twenty-four hours after surgery. The post-mortem revealed that he had thrombosis. He was only thirty nine. He is survived by his wife Juliet and their children, Rhoda Nabadda and Martin Ntale.

A courageous person who ventured into many endeavours, Peter was talented, practical and industrious. He proved what his father predicted when Peter was a teen, "This one will never be an employee, he will be a manager and employer." Lively and friendly like his siblings, Peter Martin was helpful and generous to all. He was fun to be around, having a great sense of humour, and had many friends.

Martin was greatly missed by his professional colleagues and fellow Rotarians who gave him a posthumous award, which they brought to me. It still hangs in my bedroom.

Chapter 17

My Involvement in Kiboga

In December 1986, I reoccupied our family home and, once again, became a resident of Kiboga. As I got involved in the daily lives of the people, I quickly noted that there was so much deprivation. Apart from poverty, deep apathy was real – the result of Amin's rule and wartime experiences. All the same, the people were cheerful due to the renewed hope that had been ushered in by the new government.

As I mentioned earlier, I had made up my mind not to involve myself in politics again. However, I soon realised that it would be hard to settle down happily with so many social challenges staring me in the face. I had learnt, in my social studies course in Edinburgh, that social and economic advancement requires political engagement and intervention. Social services such as schools and health care were badly lacking and many schools had no roofs and were uninhabitable. There were many orphans being cared for by overburdened relatives and neighbours and they became my priority.

Uganda Women's Effort to Save Orphans

In early 1987, I invited two women, Alex Nabakka and Victoria Kivumbi to my house to discuss the unprecedented plight of orphans. When I asked them about the situation, they responded in unison, "There are very many". I asked them to try and establish the approximate number in six or seven schools so that we could figure out if the problem required an organised approach.

I was given the figure of about 300 orphans in seven primary schools. Armed with these figures, I got in touch with the Uganda Women's Effort to Save Orphans (UWESO) headquarters in Kampala. This is a relief agency that was started in May 1986 by Mrs Janet Museveni, the President's wife, to assist children who were victims of the 1980s civil war and the HIV and AIDS epidemic. The organisation worked with community members who were organised into self-help community clusters that helped identify potential beneficiaries. Thus the grassroots networks, enhanced a sense of ownership of UWESO programmes. Although initially, services were limited to the war-torn areas of the Luweero Triangle, UWESO activities eventually spread countrywide.

Alex Nabakka travelled with me to Kampala to the UWESO headquarters, where we presented our petition. It was determined that Kiboga qualified to be a branch and before long, an interim committee for the Kiboga UWESO was created. In November, the branch was opened by Janet Museveni. She travelled in a bus full of UWESO executive members who brought with them a sizeable supply of clothing and food to distribute among orphans and their guardians. We were greatly encouraged by Mrs Museveni's commitment when she attended what became our first fundraising. This marked the beginning of my serious involvement with the community.

The management committee at Kiboga was composed of nine members with Joyce Wamara as Chairperson, Restie Nakiryowa (Secretary), Alex Nabakka (Treasurer) and Joyce Kiiza (Assistant Treasurer). I was the Co-ordinator and the other members were H. Katuramu, F. Nantaba, Teddy Nakanwagi, and Teopista Nabawanuka. Although I worked closely with them and the UWESO headquarters, I decided not to take up a leadership position because I wanted the women to learn leadership and management skills so that they could work even in my absence. As we discussed starting a project, Alex Nabakka took the initiative and identified a site on public land at Seesa Village, about four miles from Kiboga town. We approached the Assistant District Administrator, Sula Serunjogi, who allowed us to lease ten acres. Alex Nabakka paid UShs 100,000 for the lease of the land and in September 1990, the Kiboga Branch held a fundraiser at the site. We raised about 1.6 million shillings (over US$3,200 at the time) and we also received building materials for the construction of a school. Joan Kategaya represented Janet Museveni at the fundraiser and laid the school's foundation stone. By May 1992, we had finished putting up a primary school with semi-permanent structures at Seesa.

At the school, apart from formal academic studies, we established a syllabus that focused on vocational training courses in carpentry, brick making and tailoring for boys and girls – especially those who had missed out on primary school education. Agriculture skills training were also emphasised.

In December 1992, we published a fundraising booklet titled, 'Kiboga UWESO Primary School for Orphans: Give an Orphan an Education and a Future'. The booklet was sold at two fundraising occasions. We also sent it to friends within and outside Uganda, especially the UK. Our efforts were rewarded when some pupils in Cambridge, England, sacrificed their lunch money and sent £250 through my friends Sue and Peter Woodsford. Other students sent £247 through my friend Stella Goldman. We also received some cheques from well-wishers. Although the sums of money appeared small, we were greatly encouraged by the support that made it possible for us to purchase the equipment that was required at the school. Another organisation in England, Work Aid, sent a consignment of sewing machines and carpentry tools. Their contribution was handled by my daughter, Veronica, who was working in London at the time.

The school also enrolled children who were living with their parents and this enabled the orphans to mix with parented children, thus reducing the stigma of being orphaned. It also saved many other children from walking the long distances to formal government schools. In addition, parented children paid a fee that contributed to the school's income. This worked well as the parental support contributed to the development and welfare of the school.

In the midst of the school's development, a full-time social worker from the USA Peace Corps, Jackie Bye, was seconded to our branch by the UWESO head office. When she arrived, the school was still operating from a temporary building. She sent a proposal to the USA Ambassador's Fund in Kampala in which she suggested that a tangible donation would help. A donation worth UShs 10 million (US$ 8,000) was sent in the form of building materials that included cement, roofing iron sheets, timber and window shutters. The school committee and parents gave bricks, stone, sand and also paid for labour. We were then able to construct permanent buildings.

We later accepted the district administration's suggestion that the government get more involved in our school because it meant that the teachers' salaries, books and other academic materials would then be provided by the district education department. The school benefited in many ways with the district and UWESO as its joint operators. After some time, the committee handed over the school to the government as proposed by the district administration.

The Kiboga Development Association

In June 1989, an idea came to mind – the creation of a development association, a voluntary body that would help rebuild Kiboga. I reached out and shared my idea with the people I knew were born in, or were associated in one way or another with Kiboga and they thought it was a good idea. We agreed to get together and form a committee composed of concerned Kiboga citizens who lived and worked in Kampala.

Reverend Dan Kajumba was appointed chairman of the commitee and Vincent Mulindwa, vice chairman. Other officials were, Edward Katumba, Treasurer; Edward Ndaula Kawesi, Secretary; Gordon Kajumba, Publicity Secretary and Vincent Walusimbi, Youth Secretary. The committee also identified the people who dealt with sub-county responsibilities. They were: Richard Musana (Ntwetwe Sub-County), Walakira Ntwatwa (Lwamata Sub-county), Grace Sengaaga (Butemba Sub-County), Seviri Galiwango (Kiboga headquarter), Semuju L. (Bukomero Sub-County) and Retired Major Benon Biraro (Committee Member). I was on the committee as the NRC member. The Kiboga Development Association (KDA) was launched on 2nd July 1989 at the St John's Ambulance Hall in Kampala, and membership cards were issued to members.

From 1989 to 1993, KDA was involved in organising fundraisers for the rebuilding of several primary and secondary school classrooms and teachers' houses. Ssinde Primary School was KDA's first venture. Situated along the main highway from Kampala, sixteen miles from Kiboga Town, Sinde Primary School, for over fifty years, was the oldest and only school in the area. During the war, it was completely destroyed and all that was left after the roofing sheets were looted were its crumbled walls.

The rebuilding initiative was jump-started by an elder called Bukeedo, a former parent, who lived near the school. When President Museveni visited Kiboga in early February, 1986, Bukeedo, who had met the president during the war, asked him for iron sheets to rebuild the school. To make his plea even more passionate, he lay flat in the middle of the road and pointing at the ruins, he told the president, "We want iron sheets to rebuild our school." The president quickly agreed to assist. I witnessed all this as I happened to be in the president's convoy. The iron sheets were delivered as promised.

In 1989, after KDA organised a fundraiser for the materials that were required for the reconstruction, parents, pupils and teachers made the bricks and the Kiboga Sub-District Council provided the timber. With Bukeedo's iron roofing sheets, the school was completed within a short time.

In 1993, I learnt that the European Development Fund (EDF) wished to assist districts in the Luwero Triangle with facilities that had not yet been provided by the government. At the time, I was the Chairperson of the Board of Governors at Bamusuta Secondary School. The school did not have a science laboratory or library and so we applied for the EDF grant.

After a long process, the grant was given on condition that the community – school, parents and well-wishers – would contribute 25 per cent of the total cost of the project; the grant was going to cover 75 per cent. KDA spearheaded the fundraising of the 25 per cent in cash and materials. The response from the community and well-wishers was positive and we managed to raise the amount required. The construction of the science laboratory block started in 1995 and lasted three years. It was opened in December 1998 but due to the increase in enrolment at the school, the laboratory block also served as classrooms. Another science laboratory was later built by the government.

Lack of teachers' houses was another major problem in the area but fortunately, school boards and parents were also keen to address the situation. In March 1991, KDA organised a fundraiser for Bamusuta Secondary School teachers' houses and in November 1992, we organised another for Bukomero Secondary School. Each event raised enough money to construct a few teachers' houses.

In August 1990, I had the pleasure of hosting Peter and Sue Woodsford who were returning to Uganda for the first time since their departure in 1967. They visited our home in Kiboga and they demonstrated a keen interest in my social and educational activities, including the new UWESO school for orphans. Peter and Sue gave a monetary contribution that would go towards the construction of windows at the Masodde Primary School. "Use this money, which we would have paid for hotel accommodation, on your schools," they told me. Having been teachers, they were concerned about all that was required in the making of a school (the academic, functional and aesthetic aspects). They also accompanied me to a county council meeting where they keenly followed the proceedings. Later on, in 1990 and 1992, as 'Friends of Mwiri', they sent book consignments (ninety five boxes) to Busoga College Mwiri and the adjacent schools, including Kiboga schools.

Health Initiatives

Another area that KDA focused on was health services. Since the opening of Kiboga's main hospital in July 1973, the area had enjoyed having adequate health services and even during the war, it continued to function and serve the people well. However, other areas that were far from the hospital, lacked health facilities.

In the early 1990s, the Safe Motherhood Programme, an international initiative that was developed by the World Health Organization (WHO) and other agencies like the United Nations Population Fund (UNFPA), was being implemented in Uganda. It was linked to the Ministry of Health and the programme's goal was to promote reproductive health and safe motherhood practices among women, and to educate traditional birth attendants (midwives) based in rural areas that lacked modern maternity facilities.

We invited the Safe Motherhood Programme to Kiboga in July 1991 to carry out two training workshops at Ntwetwe and Lwamata sub-counties. The many attendees included mothers who used the services of traditional birth attendants in their remote communities as well as those who sought maternity services in modern health facilities.

Five months after I became the NRC representative, I was approached by an area official about the maternity centre at Bukomero, the next big trading centre after Kiboga. He informed me that although the centre had been rehabilitated by the Uganda Family Planning Association, it still lacked basic equipment including maternity beds; they needed assistance. Could I do something to make it usable?

I approached my friends, James Mulwana and Alfred Mubanda, a former schoolmate at Budo, and they generously donated basins, water cans, blankets, sugar and soap. Dr Barungi, the head of the Mubende Hospital, gave twenty beds and mattresses and enough money to buy a maternity bed for the centre. The United Pentecostal Churches International, who were building primary schools in the area, offered blankets.

The support was complemented by Dr Ronald Batta, the Deputy Minister for Health, when I telephoned him with my request for assistance. He directed his staff to give us twenty-four pairs of bed sheets, maternity kits and mackintosh sheets, among other items.

On 2nd November 1989, the maternity ward of the Bukomero Maternity Centre was opened in a ceremony that was graced by officials from the Uganda Family Planning Association. The night before the opening day, I slept in the ward on one of the beds. There was great jubilation on inauguration day and the communities around the hospital turned up in great numbers.

By the early 1990s, the HIV and AIDS epidemic had become a health and societal issue and that was how my health sector concerns extended to creating HIV and AIDS awareness in secondary schools. The scourge quickly spread throughout the country. In October 1991, I approached The AIDS Support Organisation (TASO) at Mulago Hospital and a member of staff, Mrs Margaret Ntege, was assigned to travel with me to Kiboga. We were accompanied by my brother-in-law, Dr David Sserwada (formerly of the WHO). We visited Bukomero, Bamusuta, Vvumba, and Nankandula secondary schools where Mrs Ntege and Dr Sserwada facilitated HIV and AIDS awareness discussions which were much appreciated by teachers and students.

Industrial Training

Many youths had dropped out of school during the war and they had no marketable skills, no exposure to the world outside Kiboga, and no idea of what they wanted to do. The situation after the war was that they ran a high risk of falling into bad behaviour and becoming aimless citizens. Having experienced violence, they could easily engage in crime.

I was aware that many Kiboga people were concerned about the youth and some were doing something about it. Seviri Galiwango, a resident of Kiboga and a KDA member, had already organised the training of youth in small-scale industrial skills. The training was carried out by the Uganda Small Scale Industries Association (USSIA) which was already operating in Kiboga. The main industries included tailoring, brick making, carpentry, basket weaving, mat making and doormat making. The youth were enthusiastic and their products were of good quality.

I knew that one of USSIA's objectives was to support and empower small-scale industrial development in small towns and rural areas. I was also aware that the USSIA was working with the Friedrich-Ebert Stifung (FES), a German not-for-profit political foundation that supported youth activities and promoted leadership skills.

We invited the FES and the USSIA headquarter staff to Kiboga. I was assisted in organising the visit by Sophia

Nabukera and Seviri Galiwango, USSIA staff members in Kiboga, and Margaret Ndekera, the Secretary General of the East African Confederation of Small Scale Industries, who worked with the two organisations.

In August 1989, FES and USSIA visited Kiboga and met the district leaders. Afterwards, FES visited the youth in their various small scale industries workshops. Many of the youth were inspired by the visit, especially when they realised that the productive enterprises they were engaging in would contribute to enhancing their livelihoods.

Women Skills Enhancement

I have always known and believed that to build a firm foundation when developing a community, one must first 'develop' the women in it. With that in mind, I thought that enrollment in short courses to enhance knowledge and skills that improve the quality of their daily lives and farming activities would be beneficial for the women of Kiboga.

The Ministry of Agriculture had already started conducting short residential home economics and agriculture courses and therefore, when I approached the ministry, my request for a seminar was welcomed and a two-day course was organised in 1994. One hundred women from all over the district attended the training at the County hall. There being no accommodation, they brought along their personal bedding that consisted of mats and blankets, and slept on the floor at the venue. Feedback from the women indicated that they appreciated the experience and they thought that the training was practical and informative.

International Women's Day

I learnt that Women's Day on 8th March has its origins in Eastern Europe, where women used to work under harsh conditions. In Uganda, the International Women's Day was first observed in 1985 and in 1989, parliament declared the day a public holiday. Although a national celebration was in place, I thought it necessary to organise annual celebrations in Kiboga to inspire women and help them understand what Women's Day was all about.

Local leaders were involved in organising the celebrations that were rotated every year to different sub-county headquarters. In 1990, the event was hosted at the Bukalamuli Catholic Mission School; in 1991, at the Kiboga headquarters; in 1992, at Bukomero sub-county; in 1993, at Butemba sub-county; in 1994, at Ntwetwe sub-county and in 1995, at the Kiboga headquarter. The Women's Days events inspired and united the women in the counties who realised that progress would only come their way if they worked together. During the celebrations, women showcased their handicrafts and agricultural products and entertained participants with song and dance.

Electricity

Finally, I turned my attention to the area's electricity supply. Before the war, the main electricity transformer at Bukomero Trading Centre supplied an area stretching about 100 miles along the Kampala-Hoima Highway through Kiboga town. During the conflict, it was destroyed along with the town's other infrastructures. In 1989, three years after the war, the supply had not been fully restored and all the small trading centres were still in total darkness. I approached the concerned authorities about the problem and they explained that although they understood the urgency, they faced many obstacles and it would take time to resolve the problem. Eventually, after about a year, the transformer problem was resolved.

The Creation of Kiboga District

Kiboga was one of the ten sub-counties in the Singo County of the Buganda Kingdom. Around 1975, in a new central government structure, Kiboga was made a sub-district of Mubende District. By 1980, Kiboga elders started demanding that their sub-district be upgraded to a district.

Becoming a full district meant independence and the ability to get income from taxes and transfers from the central government as well as deciding how to best use the funds. Self government also made for better administration and social services, and having control over an area's rate of development.

When President Museveni visited Kiboga in February 1986, he was met by a big gathering and a memorandum was read. One of the main requests was that the sub-district be elevated to a full district. By 1989, more sub-districts in the country were demanding district status. In 1990, the Kiboga sub-district council, led by its chairman, Fred Semaganda, a former Mayor of Kampala, and the vice chairman, Joseph Sematte, renewed and spearheaded the demand for the district status. The council appointed a committee consisting of Joseph Sematte, Siriri Kyeyune, Francis Bajabayira, Dr Godfrey Kiyingi, Rajab Ssali and myself, to research on the issue and prepare a memorandum.

One morning in early January 1991, the Minister for Local Government, Jaberi Bidandi Ssali, called me and demanded that a memorandum on Kiboga be sent to him as soon as possible. When I relayed the message to the committee, Fred Semaganda suggested that I work with him at his home in Kansanga in Kampala to complete it. I read the report out as he typed on his manual typewriter. I still remember the nice lunch his wife Beatrice prepared for us as we worked.

The memorandum had to illustrate clearly why the mother district could no longer offer adequate services, and prove that the existing sub-county facilities could support a district. Our memorandum outlined the communication problems caused by the long distance and bad roads between the Mubende District Headquarters and the Kiboga Sub-District. It also pointed out that Kiboga had a big referral hospital and structures that were suitable for district offices and that the area had a large population with a base of potential taxpayers. The memorandum was ready by the end of the day and the following morning, I sent it to the minister.

On 15th March 1991, the resolution was presented and passed in the NRC and the sub-districts of Kiboga, Kalangala, Kisoro, Kibaale and Pallisa became districts. I was absent from parliament during that historic session because we had buried my mother the previous day. That evening, I was at my sister Janet Mdoe's home with family members when I heard the good news on the radio. To my family's surprise, I shouted with delight – in the midst of a sombre environment. When I told them the good news, they all shared in my joy.

The creation of Kiboga District and, ten years later, the elevation of its trading centre to a township, opened the doors to development in the area. The first benefits after the elevation included the tarmacking of the Busunju-Kiboga part of the Kampala-Hoima Road, the building of more health centres and schools and an increase in electricity connectivity.

The latter led to the opening up of more trading centres and, thus, enhanced commercial activity. Kiboga was rising again.

* * *

I have been able to relate my activities in Kiboga and recall the people with whom I worked because I kept diaries and recorded details of all key events as they occurred. I believe in the Latin phrase which I have often quoted: *Verba volant, scripta manent* (spoken words fly away, written words remain). I hope this history of Kiboga and the revival of its schools and other infrastructure will benefit current and future generations in Kiboga and the rest of Uganda.

Chapter 18

Rekindling My Involvement in the Women's Movement

In the 1970s, President Idi Amin abolished all the women's organisations that were not faith-based. As mentioned earlier, the Uganda Council of Women (UCW), our flagship organisation, was a victim of the ban. After Idi Amin's ouster and the violence that followed, it was impossible to revive the women organisations. However, by God's grace, the vision and mission of the various original groups did not die.

The revival of the women's movement can be traced back to the United Nations (UN) Women's Decade Conference that was held in Nairobi in 1985. Strengthened by the conference, the idea of women empowerment quickly spread among young educated women in Uganda, especially university graduates. Although they operated under different organisations, they all upheld the determination, mission and vision of the women from earlier decades.

Ten years after the Nairobi conference, the 1995 UN Women's Decade Conference that was held in Beijing was an even greater inspiration. It was attended by several women MPs and women movement leaders, including Rebecca Mulira, a founder member of the 1950s UCW. After the Beijing

Conference, there was a burst of action and the formation of several women's non-government organisations.

Action for Development

One of the first new generation women's organisations I got involved in was Action for Development (ACFODE). In 1989, when I joined the NRC, I met Miria Matembe, one of the ACFODE pioneers. Her fiery inspiration and ACFODE's commitment to extending the organisation's activities to rural areas attracted me to the organisation. The spirit of the original women's movements was strongly embedded in ACFODE

Inspired by some of the ideas at the UN Women's Conference in Nairobi in July 1985, ACFODE was launched in November of the same year with the core purpose of empowering women and influencing legislation on gender equality through advocacy. The organisation also advocated good governance and accountability and the prevention of violence against women. In addition, their work involved the enhancement of women's capabilities – to enable them manage their own affairs and stand up for their rights in their communities.

One of ACFODE's first undertakings was the regular production of *Arise*, a magazine that was widely read. It deliberately set out to be an inspirational publication. The publication highlighted the organisation's activities and discussed the aspirations of women.

In 2000, ACFODE started assessing people's lives in rural communities and studying women's cultural attitudes to try and figure out how best to run local programmes in order to maximise the impact of the desired outcomes. The team's thinking was that there was a need to prepare the ground before any programme ideas were implemented because any sudden changes imposed on the rural women, and the community in general, could result in culture shocks. Therefore, a 'Change Process Team' was created in 2001.

I admired this approach as it ensured that both ACFODE and the women beneficiaries understood each other – a necessity, especially because of the academic gap that existed between the ACFODE members and the rural women. Since the possibilities and advantages of the programme were studied first, this created trust and ensured that the women participated in something that they understood and valued, and this contributed to the success of the programme.

In May 2002, ACFODE was launched in Kiboga District. The memorable launch was widely publicised through banners that were placed around the trading centre and its surroundings. It took centre stage in the whole town. The women marched on the main road, enthuthiastically waving placards and banners.

Right from the start, ACFODE focused on involving women who never had the benefit of going to school – or had only completed primary school – in the organisation's activities. Great effort was also directed at identifying local women leaders whose critical role would be to determine future programmes in ACFODE's areas of operation. The grass-rootedness was a unique characteristic of ACFODE and the reason why its programmes had great impact and success in communities.

Although I did not hold any leadership position in the area after I retired from parliament, being a member of women organisations gave me the opportunity to continue being involved in leading the many programmes ACFODE and other women organisations brought to Kiboga. The work of these women's organisations complemented much of the very work that I had been involved in for many years and I was, therefore, happy and fulfilled. Looking ahead, I could see the women's movements progressing with increasing power, to impact future generations.

Forum for Women in Democracy

The Forum for Women in Democracy (FOWODE) has a foundation story that is different from all the other women organisations. Its roots are totally indigenous. It was started by a group of women delegates during the Constituent Assembly (CA) of 1994 to 1995. The idea was initiated by a delegate in the CA, Winnie Byanyima, the MP for Mbarara Municipality. One day, at the end of a session, she invited me and eight other women delegates to a meeting. The others were Solome Mukisa, Tezira Jamwa, Benigna Mukiibi, Victoria Sebagereka, Betty Akech Okullu, Esther Dhugira Opoti, Margaret Ziwa, and Loice Bwambale.

At the meeting, Winnie pointed out that there was a critical need for Ugandan women to become conversant with democratic politics. In the constitution-making environment that we were involved in, we had all noted that there was a deficiency in this area. It therefore took very little to convince us that we needed to organise ourselves to address the issue. She informed us that she had already sourced funds from international organisations to finance the required activities. With such a timely opportunity, by mid-afternoon, right there, in a small room in the International Conference Centre, FOWODE was born.

FOWODE's vision is, *'A just and fair society where women and men participate equally and benefit from decision-making processes'*. I have always believed that focusing exclusively on women would limit the intended results because the roles of women and men are inextricably interwoven. FOWODE's vision promised better outcomes of women's development because it has always been clear that when men and women participate equally and compete on equal ground, the results are better for society at large.

After the 1995 constitution was promulgated, the CA wound up its business but parliament continued sitting. Since we were all still in parliament, we took the opportunity to strengthen our newborn FOWODE.

In the discussions, we discovered the various shortcomings that we had as women in politics, including the fact that most women participated in the political process at various levels, with low economic, social, and political awareness. As a result women had limited understanding of how these factors affected citizens and what it takes to make impactful decisions and policies.

FOWODE's approach to political participation was new to most young female politicians. They were empowered when they learnt how to consider and debate wider issues of economic, social and political value – a move that enhanced their decision-making capabilities.

I had identified young, educated women leaders with potential who could replace me in my home district. These were Mary Margaret Nalugo, who was elected to parliament in 1992, and Ruth Nankabirwa Sentamu, who was elected to the CA in 1994 and, thereafter, to parliament in 1996. Both were Makerere University graduates. By this time, the 'affirmative action' slots that were created for women in parliament had been written into the new constitution. This created opportunities for more women to represent districts, municipalities and people with disability, among other sectors in society.

Soon after the new Parliament was formed (after I retired), FOWODE organised an induction workshop for fifty-six women MPs and it was held from the 28th to the 29th of July 1996 under the theme, 'Creating Effective Leadership'. I was not aware that my participation in the women's emancipation struggle had been noted until I received an invitation from Winnie Byanyima, the FOWODE Chairperson, to the closing ceremony of the induction workshop, where I would be honoured.

At the ceremony, a long tribute from FOWODE was read by Ruth Nankabirwa Sentamu, the young parliamentarian from Kiboga. It read in part:

> ...Rhoda, a leader who has inspired and benefitted women of all ages and backgrounds and contributed tremendously to the cause of gender equality. FOWODE recognises you, Rhoda N. N. Kalema, as a transformative leader of vision, commitment, courage and compassion.

I was humbled by the tribute. Today, the lovely certificate I received hangs in my study.

One of FOWODE's goals was to enhance women's leadership skills through intergenerational learning and constant training, and the organisation's recognition challenged me to continue mentoring intergenerational women. In July 2008, I was invited to close the 5th Mentorship Camp for young women leaders. I was excited when I realised that FOWODE's vision and mission was still being pursued aggressively by the young leaders, thirteen years since the birth of the organisation.

In March 2012, I was invited again by FOWODE on International Women's Day to dialogue with young people and share my experiences in promoting women's rights. The day's theme was, 'Connecting Girls; Inspiring Cultures'. They hung onto my stories dating back to the 1960s when I was in my thirties, and among the youngest in the women's movement. They took in my experiences with the NRC and the CA, when at 67, I was the oldest in the group.

In 2002, FOWODE organised a retreat for women leaders with the objective of getting them to tell their life stories including how they achieved their leadership status. Their stories were published in two books. The first, *Uganda Women in Public Life,* is a photobook record of women leaders and it was exhibited at the Nommo Gallery in Kampala in May and June, 2002. The second book, *A Rising Tide: Uganda Women's Struggle for a Public Voice,* contains thirty-four stories in four sections that cover different generations. The narrators, women from diverse social and economic backgrounds, have one thing in common – each broke through barriers and challenges in her personal life and career to become a leader. The stories also illustrate how those with formal education opened the gate for those who did not have that advantage, so they too, could progress. This 'opening the gate' is well explained by Pumla Kisosonkole's statement on becoming the first African woman in the LegCo in 1956. She stated: "You know, when a door has been opened for one person, that person should put her foot down there and let the door remain open until all the others are in … to bring the others forward".[22]

22 Quoted in Aili Mari Tripp's, Women and Politics in Uganda (Madison: University of Wisconsin Press, 2000), p. 29.

Forum for African Women Educationalists – Uganda

I came across the Forum for African Women Educationalists – Uganda (FAWE-U), in the early 2000s. FAWE is a Pan-African non-governmental organisation that was formed in 1993 in Nairobi. It is the fruit of five visionary African women ministers for education who convened to address the appalling state of girls' education in Africa. Believing that the girl child needed a special push if the wide gender gap in education was to be closed, their goal was to accelerate female participation in education at all levels.

FAWE's Uganda chapter was launched in 1997 in Kampala – a joint effort between the Ministry of Education, Makerere University, non-governmental organisations, and individuals who were committed to addressing gender parity in education. The founders were Florence Sembatya, Ann Galiwango, Ruth Nvumetta Kavuma, Joyce Mpanga, and Florence Kanyike. FAWE-U's mission was in line with the original aim of the Uganda Council of Women – the fulfilment of our long-held desire – women's emancipation. I believe that educated girls and women accelerate development in any society. Hence the often quoted adage: "Educate a man and you educate an individual; educate a woman and you educate a nation."

For about twenty years, I served on the governing boards of several rural secondary schools in Kiboga where I observed that there were fewer girls in all the institutions.

When I became the NRC representative for Kiboga, one of the first things I did was to visit all the local schools. At Vvumba Primary School, whereas the number of girls in Primary One and Two was almost equal to boys, their numbers reduced with each succeeding year as they moved to higher classes. By Primary Seven, there were very few girls left. This pattern was repeated in most of the schools; in fact, the story was the same all over the country.

The main reason for this drop-out rate seems to be that the girl child's education is ranked very low when it comes to prioritising family finances. The cultural requirement that girls stay at home to carry out household chores also interferes with their schooling. While there are many other reasons, the basic one, I believe, is uneducated parents, especially mothers, who do not value their daughters' education.

One day, about 2003, after chairing a school board meeting, one board member who was a parent at the school approached me. He told me that one of his daughters had been assisted with school fees by an organisation called FAWE. He asked, "Can my other daughter also be registered for financial assistance by the same organisation?"

Although the man looked reasonably successful, owned a small grocery shop in town and was a responsible parent who served on the school board without pay (like everyone else), he could not afford to send his intelligent daughters to the schools that matched their abilities.

I had known about FAWE, but this was the first time that I became aware of the organisation's impact. I decided to visit them in their Kampala office.

As I got acquainted with FAWE-U's objectives and mission, I liked what I heard. For a girl to receive financial assistance, she had to be an academic achiever, be admitted to a secondary school and have a genuine financial need. I realised that FAWE-U was another avenue for women empowerment and I signed up immediately as a member.

At the time, FAWE-U was already expanding across the whole country, identifying districts where the girls' education required urgent intervention. A pilot project was planned for Kiboga and a few other districts.

In July 2006, FAWE-U launched the pilot project in the remote Bisiika Primary School. Professor Mary Okwakol led a powerful FAWE-U team and I was the chief guest at the event that was graced by many primary and secondary schools. The occasion also brought together school teachers, parents, district officials, and community leaders. A variety of activities, presentations and exhibitions were showcased and it turned out to be a happy day for the entire community. I had never witnessed such enthusiasm over girls' education before. Girls were given items that they could not afford, including exercise books, pens and more importantly, sanitary towels which ensured that they did not miss or drop out of school. That day, many people registered as members of FAWE-U.

FAWE-U's scholarship scheme is supported by international, regional, and local organisations. At the 2009 Annual General Meeting and dinner, it was noted that seven girls who were supported by FAWE-U had graduated from university. That was just the start. The number of beneficiaries has grown and it is encouraging to see that many FAWE-U beneficiaries are giving back and continuing the tradition of supporting others alongside the organisations that supported them.

In order to inspire young women, FAWE-U started a programme where the organisation awarded young girls that they recognised as 'models of excellence,' including girls educated outside their programmes. That was how my daughter, Dr Gladys Kalema, the first wildlife veterinary doctor in Uganda, received an award in 1999. At the time, she was working for the Uganda Wildlife Authority.

Membership with Other Women Organisations

I have been associated with other women's organisations, including the Women International Cross-Cultural Exchange (Isis-WICCE), Federación Internacional de Abogadas (FIDA-U) and the Uganda Women's Network (UWONET) and they all deserve a mention.

Isis-WICCE, is named after Isis, the Egyptian goddess of creativity, knowledge and wisdom. The organisation was founded in Geneva in 1974 and it moved its headquarters to Uganda in 1993 to emphasise its commitment to women in countries in the southern hemisphere. This commitment is reflected in its projects at the national, regional, and international levels.

My introduction to Isis-WICCE was via a letter from the Executive Director, Milicent Aligaweesa, informing me that they had decided to recognise me as a woman activist and that, because the organisation was a documentation centre, they wanted to capture the lead provided by the Ministry of Gender and Community Development by putting together a record of women achievers in Uganda. In March 1997, I was given a silver shield for the Top Woman Achiever's Award for 1996-97 at the Grand Imperial Hotel in Kampala. In my appreciation speech, I promised to work with them whenever they needed my support. MP Miria Matembe received the second Achievers Award, and MP Baba Diri, a blind lady who was also a member of parliament (representing people living with disability), received the third award.

I was attracted by Isis-WICCE's agenda that focused on girls' and women's emancipation and leadership, and I showed up whenever I was invited to meetings and trainings. Even more important was their focus on issues that impacted on women, girls, and children negatively, including rape, violence, and armed conflict. This new focus only developed in the last few decades; it was rare in earlier years.

FIDA-U, an Association of Women Lawyers, is an affiliate of the International Federation of Women Lawyers that was founded in 1944 in Mexico. Since then, FIDA has established membership in more than seventy countries around the world.

In Uganda, FIDA was established in 1974 by a group of women lawyers, with the aim of promoting human rights, especially the rights of women and children. The founders included Joyce Katende, Eva Mulira, Justice Leticia Kikonyogo, Justice Alice Mpagi, and Solome Kalule. They were later joined by Justice Mary Maitum, Rebecca Kadaga, Sarah Bagalaliwo, Justice Anna Magezi, Christina Kaluma, Miria Matembe, and Justice Ruth Masika. The first legal aid clinic that was established to help local women access justice, was set up in 1988.

I became interested in FIDA-U when I heard about their programmes that educated women on laws related to marriage and inheritance, especially how they affected children.

Around 1991, when I asked FIDA-U to visit my rural home area and introduce their services, they obliged and they held a session in Bukwiri Township. At first, many men and women turned up. However, since some of the valuable subjects touched on sensitive cultural issues, such as marriage laws, the men were not comfortable and one by one, they withdrew from the meeting. Eventually, mostly women and the male official who had convened the event were left. I learnt afterwards that the women were told by their husbands never to attend the meetings as FIDA-U would 'confuse and mislead' them.

Perhaps I was too enthusiastic and I forgot that 'old habits die hard'. I should have prepared the people better about FIDA-U's work. I did not attempt to invite FIDA-U to other areas because I knew the reception would be the same. However, my faith in FIDA-U never wavered and I continued to call on their services when necessary.

The Uganda Women's Network

In October 2012, when Uganda commemorated fifty years of independence, the Uganda Women's Network (UWONET), an umbrella women's organisation with over sixteen organisations affiliated to it, also celebrated women's contributions since independence by organising a national Women's Week at the Hotel Africana in Kampala. The theme was, 'Uganda Women Can', which is also UWONET's motto.

That week, I participated in two panel discussions, alongside many organisations and individuals who discussed their work and displayed their crafts. The week ended with a dinner that was organised by UWONET and the Uganda Women's Parliamentary Association (UWOPA) at the Sheraton Hotel. President Yoweri Museveni was the chief guest. I was among the many women who were recognised for their contributions to society. I received a Lifetime Achiever's Award for, I was told, "Outstanding contributions in enhancing women's empowerment."

I was invited to give the vote of thanks to the President and I reminded everyone that the 'Women's Week' was a great honour to all the women who founded and carried the movement forward. I also noted that the achievements and spirit of the women's movement fifty years after independence, and ninety-eight years since its beginning with the Mothers' Union in 1914, reflected a successful journey.

I added that the women of today believe that 'United Women Can' because the women of the past had succeeded by working together and that their unity and common purpose had enabled us to create a strong movement. I mentioned some courageous and selfless women from the past from the various regions of Uganda, including Elizabeth Kanyamunyu from Mbarara, Irene Emulu from Soroti, Janet Oryema from Gulu, Lakeri Kadama from Busoga, Janet Wesonga from Mbale, Marjorie Kabuzi and Edith Katama from Toro, Rebecca Mulira, Hannah Lule and Eseza Makumbi from Buganda, and Sarah Ntiro from Bunyoro. The president also received an award for his unwavering support for women's leadership.

I am pleased that I have lived to see the development of the women's movement and the level it has achieved. In the early years, we fought for basic social justice – we yearned to be recognised as equals with men in society, at the very least.

Looking ahead into the 21st Century, I am excited about the new generation of women's organisations. The majority sprouted after the 1980s and their emergence was like a colourful picture of sprouting seeds and greenery in a tropical scenario at the onset of rains, following a severe drought, or the coming up of spring flowers after a harsh winter. With these images in mind, one thing is clear to me: the current women's organisations have carried on the vision and mission of the original movement because the concerns are still the same; the progress of girls and women in the areas of social justice, education, health, politics, economics, and gender equality.

I have had the great privilege of being a bridge between the old and new organisations, and I salute the common determination, mission and vision that links all women across the decades.

Chapter 19

Engaging With the Bible Society and the Scripture Union

My retirement from active politics also enabled me to get more involved in two ministries that I am passionate about: the Bible Society and the Scripture Union. This is in addition to the demands on my time by my beloved Kiboga, my children, grandchildren, and the wider family.

The Bible Society

In 1977, I became a member of the Bible Society. Among the expectations is that members will offer their time and talent to fundraise and to strengthen the translation and distribution of Bibles. I first served on its executive committee but when I joined the National Consultative Council (NCC) in 1979, although I was a life member, I stopped participating in the society's activities.

In early 1990, I received a letter from the Campus Crusade for Christ organisation in the USA through the local Lay Involvement For Evangelism (LIFE) Ministry, inviting me to serve as one of the 1,000 Christian leaders from around the world on the International Committee of Reference for New

Life 2000. That was the *'Help Change the World through New Life by the Year 2000'* project, that was designed to introduce the Gospel to at least one billion people by the year 2000.

I viewed the invitation as a divine responsibility. However, I realised that it was too late for me to adjust my commitments, which I would have to do to carry out, effectively, the significant role of getting to the universally targeted population of one billion. I even considered joining a theological or Bible college, but that plan was not practical – also due to my family commitments. I prayed for guidance on how I could join the crusade in a practical way. The guidance I received pointed me towards pursuing the strategy through an active membership with the Bible Society.

That was how, in 1996, upon leaving active politics, I resumed my participation in the Bible Society and registered to be on the women's task force that was involved in voluntary fundraising. God then revealed to me that if more people could access the Gospel through reading personal copies of the scriptures, it would be a great start to fulfilling the New Life 2000's goals.

While introducing the Scripture Union in one of the schools in Kiboga one day, I asked the assembled secondary school students how many owned a Bible. In a gathering of about ninety students, only one boy raised his hand and told me that he had a Bible that he borrowed from his father. I also discovered that the Christians in my church – the Anglican Church – and in other churches in my home area, did not own Bibles. I found out that was due to three reasons. Firstly, literacy was very low among the many who went to church and secondly, the church leadership did not do much to help Christians access the Word of God through reading the Bible.

Lastly, most of the older congregants had eye problems that had not been addressed. I, therefore, started buying Bibles in bulk from the Bible House in Kampala and delivering them to Christians and students, at the 'distribution price' – without making any profit.

It was a rewarding exercise, especially when I started receiving telephone calls and people coming to my home to enquire about buying Bibles for themselves, their children or for confirmation candidates. Through volunteering my time, I have come to love and value the Bible even more and I have grown in the spirit.

Over the centuries, ordinary men and even kings took the trouble to translate and print versions of the Bible in different languages and I have always wondered, "Why did they do it?" My brief answer to my own question is: "So that men, women, young people and children may seek and receive guidance on how to live their lives well and determine where they will end up." I like the way William Lyon Phelps (1865-1943), a professor from Yale University, put it when he revealed, "I thoroughly believe in a university education for both men and women; but I believe a knowledge of the Bible without a college course is more valuable than a college course without the Bible."

Two Christian men from the past greatly influenced my involvement in distributing the Bible. The first was William Tyndale (1494-1536) and the second was Andrew van der Bijl. William Tyndale was a leader in the Protestant Reformation Movement and the priest and scholar who translated the Bible from the Greek and the Hebrew languages into English so that the common people could understand it – an illegal act in England at the time. He was betrayed, strangled and burnt

International Women's Day, Bukomero, 1992

With members of the school building committee at Bamusuta
Primary School, Kiboga. Prime Minister Samson Kisekka is 3rd from
right, Fred Semaganda is 1st left, early 1990s

Bricks made by women to build a UWESO school in Seesa. With
Rosalind Boyd from Canada and Alex Nabakka, mid 1990s

Receiving books for Kiboga schools from Peter and Sue Woodsford,
1993

Members of Committee Number Five of the Constituent Assembly at the Conference Centre. Standing R-L: 1st Rhoda Kalema, Winne Byanyima, Chairman of the CA James Wapakhabulo (in the middle with grey suit and striped tie), 1995

Signing the constitution, 1995

With Hamim Sentongo (right), campaigning in the 2001 general elections

With RDC Katenda Luutu and Assistant RDC Kagulire, inspecting Busunju-Hoima Road construction equipment at Kiboga Town, 2002

Science Laboratory Block, Bumusuta Secondary School

With Students at Kiboga Scripture Union Branch, 2005

Receiving Isis-WICCE's award from Janet Mukwaya, Minister of Gender, Labour and Social Development, 1997

As recipient of the Sudreau Global Justice Lifetime Achievement Award from Pepperdine University, School of Law and the Uganda Judiciary, May 2018

Mrs Museveni (centre), US Ambassador, Deborah R. Malac, 2nd from right and Chief Justice, Bart Katureebe pose with some of the recipients

As joint chief guests with Joyce Mpanga (3rd from right on front row) at the launch of report on gender and elections in the 2016 general election event officiated by the Swedish Ambassador

Women's Situation Room, Uganda 2016 elections

At the Old City Caesarea Gallery, Israel with Adelina Lubogo, 2010

The East African Revival Cathederal
Gahini, 2019

Leaving 'The Empty Tomb',
Israel, 2010

at the stake on 6th October 1536. Among his other crimes was that he constantly disagreed with the Church hierarchy. It is reported that as he was dying, he prayed, "Lord open the King of England's eyes." In 1539, just three years after his death, his prayer was answered. King Henry VIII authorised the publication of the English 'Great Bible' version based on Tyndale's work. It formed the basis of all subsequent English translations, including the King James Version of 1611 and that is why Tyndale is known as the 'father of the English Bible.'

On 15th July 2011, I attended a celebration that marked 400 years of the King James Version of the Bible (1611-2011) at the Uganda Bible House. Uganda's Prime Minister, Professor Apolo Nsibambi, who was chief guest, told the story behind the King James Version and that is how I was inspired to read more about the history of the Bible and William Tyndale. By 2020, the Bible Society of Uganda had translated the Bible into twenty Ugandan languages.

Andrew van der Bijl, or Brother Andrew, was a Dutch Christian who was born in the Netherlands in 1923. He is popularly known as 'God's Smuggler' which is also the title of a book that he wrote in the 1960s. *God's Smuggler* was first published in 1968 and by September 1977, it was in its thirtieth reprint. By 2016, it had sold over seventeen million copies and had been translated into thirty-five languages. In the book, he tells how he smuggled Bibles into Communist countries at the height of the Cold War – particularly to Yugoslavia and the Soviet Union. All those who have read *God's Smuggler* can never forget his famous prayer: "Lord, in my luggage I have Scriptures that I want to take to your children across this border. When you were on earth, you made the blind eyes see. Now, I pray, make seeing eyes blind. Do not let the guards see those things you do not want them to see." Amazingly, the guards never found the Bibles that he smuggled across the Yugoslav border in 1957. God answered Brother Andrew's many prayers and masses behind the Iron Curtain accessed the Word.

After learning about so many brave believers, like 'God's Smuggler,' I have often said to myself, "If I have so many witnesses who have faced extremely difficult and dangerous circumstances; today, in this 21st Century, I do not have any excuse for not witnessing for Christ."

Scripture Union

From 1987 to 2009, I was a board member, of Bukomero and Bamusuta Secondary schools. The longer I served on the boards of these schools in the rural areas, the more keenly I felt the absence of scriptural knowledge. I learnt from my social studies course that adolescence is the most difficult stage in human development. Therefore, it is important that young people get exposed to the scriptures during these critical years.

One Saturday afternoon, towards the end of 2001, I was walking in Kiboga town when I saw a vehicle moving down the street playing loud music and on top of it, were a number of young half-naked, very jovial, dancing girls. From the vehicle, a loud announcement was promoting the 'greatest entertainment ever' that would be hosted that evening at a certain venue in town. That kind of 'entertainment', with all its related vices, I got to learn, had already turned many students in secondary schools and even younger children into regular clients of the evening entertainment centres that had become big business in town. Parents appeared helpless and the town administrators and police did not seem bothered.

I could clearly see the looming danger that awaited these young people and society at large, and I was very concerned. I realised that they needed to be equipped with scriptures from an early age so that they could learn to love God and also how to choose between right and wrong.

Elsewhere, I had heard testimonies from a steady stream of young Christians about their encounters with God at school through a group called the Scripture Union (SU). The group, which works to build young people's understanding of God, was introduced to Ugandan schools in 1963 by Mr Albert Taylor, a teacher from England who first taught at Busoga College Mwiri. I was already an adult and married by then, so I never experienced the Scripture Union teachings or guidance when I was in school. However, I realised the Scripture Union's importance and the need to introduce the group to secondary schools in Kiboga.

That was how, in early 2002, I went to the Scripture Union's headquarter in Nakulabye, Kampala and met a calm young man, Jairus Mutebe, who was the Scripture Union General Secretary. He immediately showed interest in my request. I discovered that my visit was timely because there were plans to establish a new Scripture Union region in mid-western Uganda, of which Kiboga was part. Mutebe summoned the staff in charge of programmes and 16th June 2002 was fixed as the date that the Scripture Union staff would launch a new branch in Kiboga.

Six members of staff from the Scripture Union arrived a day earlier and spent the night in my home. On the day of the launch, ten other members, including the General Secretary, and eight American visitors who had arrived in Uganda the previous day, attended the ceremony at All Saints' Church in Kiboga town. About 120 students from six schools around

Kiboga attended the event accompanied by their teachers and the local clergy. Afterwards, the students had lunch at the church and the Scripture Union staff, the clergy and the American guests had lunch at my home.

Before the arrival of the SU in schools, Christian clubs that held regular fellowship meetings during lunch breaks, already existed. Sadly, Bible reading was not emphasised by the clubs because many did not have Bibles. After the launch, the Christian clubs in the schools were renamed Scripture Union or SU Clubs and they were also established in other schools.

As the Scripture Union work in schools took root, we formed an executive committee that included volunteers and student representatives to oversee the Scripture Union's work. Every June, a one-day conference that brought together all the schools for a day of energetic singing, praying, Bible study sessions and testimonies was held. On the day, a guest speaker addressed a specific theme.

In 2009, the Scripture Union in Kiboga rented a one-room office and hired a full-time worker. In June 2010, we rented a bigger place and it was opened by the Bishop of our Mityana Diocese, Rt. Rev Bishop Stephen Kazimba Mugalu.

The Scripture Union celebrated fifteen years in Kiboga in July 2017, in an event that was attended by 285 students from fourteen schools. The feedback from participants and the large crowds was a clear indication that the whole community had been inspired by the celebration. After the event, many people who watched a video of the event revealed that they had been drawn to the scriptures by what they saw. Teachers also took an increased interest in Scripture Union activities and many schools appointed teacher patrons for their clubs. Parents paid up whenever subscription were requested because they saw the value of the Scripture Union in their teenagers' lives. During such moments, I am reminded of St Jerome (AD 347-420), who carried out research and translated a number of scripture books from Hebrew into Latin and Greek. I love his quote that states, "Ignorance of scriptures is ignorance of Christ."

I am grateful to the many people who helped us build the Kiboga Scripture Union branch during the first ten years. Dr Kenneth Marx from the USA sent me US$ 500 which was enough to buy 124 Bibles at the Bible Society shop where students bought them at a low price. Through Dr Al and Pat Rhea in the USA, Dr Stan A. Frye, the pastor of Gateway International Mission Inc. asked Reverend William Sentumbwe of Uganda Christian Light Foundation to send us 10,000 copies of the New Testament. They were given free of charge to students who attended the annual Scripture Union conferences.

I pray that my involvement in the Bible Society and the Scripture Union since 1977 will continue to 'bear fruit' – fruit that will last (John 15:16, NIV) in Kiboga and my country for generations to come.

Death of My Granddaughter Zalwango

On 30th July 2005, we had yet another family tragedy, the death of my eldest grandchild, Alice Rhoda Zalwango, who was just twenty-eight years old. Zally, as we called her, was the first born child of my daughter Betty, who died when Zally was just ten.

Zally was a quiet girl and we accepted that because we believed it was her nature. However, as she grew older, we noticed that she would suffer bouts of depression and I got her to see a psychiatrist for a period of two years. Sensible, practical and hardworking from a very young age, she scored high marks throughout all her school years. She studied architecture at Makerere and after her graduation in 2001, joined an architectural firm in Kampala, Ssentoogo and Partners, where she worked until 2003. During her time at the University, Zally used her architectural skills to design a guest house, Nakalema Guest House, at our Kiboga home.

Five weeks after she returned from her MBA degree course at Coventry University, she succumbed to a drug overdose that was triggered by depression. She died before her graduation which was unfortunate because she had longed for and worked so hard to achieve her Masters' degree. I realised, at her death, that the deep longing for her mother had been building up inside her all along and had worsened and finally overwhelmed her when she went to Coventry University.

Writing about the deaths in my family has not been easy. It has been very painful and I wish I could avoid thinking about the tragedies. But because the lives of our loved ones were a great blessing to me and my family, sadly, the grief experienced at their untimely deaths has also been part of our life and must be included in telling my life's experiences.

Through reading the Bible regularly, I have learnt and understood a lot more about suffering: that all suffering, all pain, all disappointments and emptiness is a seed. Sow all the seed of suffering in God and He will finally yield a bountiful crop of comfort and acceptance of all the difficult situations, in His time.

Chapter 20

Spiritual Tours

For a long time, I wished that I could visit Gahini in Rwanda – the birthplace of the 1935 East African Revival. Listening to and meeting so many passionate evangelists that were pioneers of the East African Revival made me believe that the spiritual atmosphere of 1935 still dwelt there. Finally, I got the chance to visit Rwanda when I attended the Rwanda Evangelical Convention that was held from 25th to 28th July 2007.

The convention was organised under the auspices of the Shyira Diocese, in Musanze, Rwanda, with Bishop John Rucyahana as the main coordinator. The convention's mission statement was, 'Rebuilding Rwanda'.

Many Rwandese were forced to flee from their country by successive political upheavals that started in the 1950s, into Uganda where they sought refuge, settled and became part of the Ugandan society. With the takeover of Rwanda's government by the Rwanda Patriotic Front in 1994, many refugees chose to return to Rwanda. Bishop Rucyahana lived in Uganda where he served in different churches and among the many friends he left in Uganda was a Rwandese couple, Reverend Emmanuel Nkuusi and his wife Joy, who live in Kiboga town. Sadly, in early 2007, the Nkuusi's lost their

18-year-old daughter after a long battle with cancer. Bishop Rucyahana, his wife Harriet and I, attended her funeral.

During the funeral, Bishop Rucyahana told me that he wanted to buy a Rwandese Bible and since I happened to have some new copies at home, I gave him one. He also asked me for two Luganda prayer books and about two months later, he went back to Rwanda.

Later in 2007, I received a message from Joy Nkuusi, and it read, "Bishop Rucyahana has invited you to attend the convention in Shyira in July and a number of people, including the Archbishop of Uganda and other bishops, have also been invited. But we (the Nkuusis) are unable to go." The invitation was a pleasant surprise. It looked like I was going to fulfill my long-time dream after all. Since 1949, Gahini had been stamped in my heart.

At first, I was anxious about travelling so far by road but since the urge to go to Rwanda for the convention was very strong, I prayed about it. I finally decided to travel by air to Kigali after Bishop Rucyahana assured me that he would send a vehicle to pick and drive me and some other guests from Kigali to Shyira. I spent a night in Kigali where I was accommodated by Rita, the niece of my great friend, Eseza Kalimuzo.

The next morning, I travelled from Kigali to Shyira, a journey of seventy miles with one of the guests. Most of the time, the weather in Rwanda was cold and I caught a bad flu. However, this did not dampen my enthusiasm. The accommodation at the Diocesan Guest House was comfortable and homely and I looked forward to the next day's convention.

The theme of the Convention, 'Go and bear fruit in keeping with repentance' (from Matthew 3:8), emphasised that Rwanda was to be rebuilt around repentance because people needed to forgive one another if the deep hatred that resulted from the 1994 genocide was to be shed.

The theme was expounded on by a number of renowned speakers including the Archbishop of Rwanda, the Most Reverend Emmanuel Kolini, the retired Archbishop of South East Asia, the Most Reverend Moses Tay, Bishops from Rwanda, the USA and two rectors from the International Anglican Church of the United States. Rwanda, they emphasised, could only be rebuilt by the people who produced fruits of forgiveness.

The speakers acknowledged that repenting the hatred that dominated their hearts would not be easy, but it was possible if they had the conviction that Jesus had died for them so that they could bear the fruit of love in their hearts.

They gave several biblical examples of repentance including King David's deep repentance for taking Bathsheba as his wife and scheming her husband's death and how he went on to be in the genealogy of Jesus Christ; Peter's repentance after denying Jesus after which he became a leader of the early church; and Paul who repented for persecuting Jesus' followers and went on to spread the Gospel around the world.

Towards the end of the convention, participants were taken on tours to meet ordinary Rwandans. I was in the group that visited prisoners who were found guilty of committing genocide. We were shocked by their stories about the in-laws and close relatives that they killed just because they were Tutsi or Hutu. The visit also turned out to be a time of praise when we witnessed how some of the prisoners were touched by the Gospel that we shared with them on repenting the sin of murder and on forgiveness.

On the last afternoon of the convention, people excitedly poured into the middle of the arena as we sang one of my favourite hymns, *"Ompise Mukama okujjanga gyoli..."* (You have called me Lord, to come to you), in Kinyarwanda and Luganda.

I still wanted to go to Gahini so I asked how I could get there. I was told that although it was not too far from Musanze, it was not that close. In the end, although I was unable to visit Gahini, I was satisfied with my experience at the Musanze convention. It was my own 'Gahini experience'. I shall carry the blessed memory till the end of my life.

In May 2015, a fundraiser was held in Kampala by the 'Friends of Gahini' towards the building of the East African Revival Cathedral, close to the site of the original Gahini Church that was built in 1922. It was the oldest Anglican Church in Rwanda. Since I could not attend the fundraiser, I sent a contribution. The new Cathedral was opened in May, 2019.

A Visit to the Holy Land

Israel was the other place that I had always wished to visit. I was mostly curious to know if the politics and geography of today's Israel were in any way similar to the Israel in the Old and New Testaments. I also wished to see with my own eyes, the historical and spiritual sites I had always read about in the Bible.

In 2010, from the 20th to the 28th of March, I was blessed when my wish came to fruition. I travelled with my good friend Adelina Lubogo in a group of about forty-five people from Kampala on a pilgrimage that was organised by the 'Christians for Israel International', based in Kampala.

We visited many important sites and what we learnt as well as the explanations that we were given about the Old Testament and the New Testament sites enriched my understanding of the Bible.

On the first day, we watched a film on Jesus' trial and sentencing before His crucifixion. We also walked along the edge of the ruins of the vast palace which was the headquarter of Pontius Pilate at Caesarea Maritima. We visited other important Bible sites and learnt about their significance including two memorable Old Testament sites. The first was, Mount Carmel that is famous for Prophet Elijah's contest with Ahab and Baal's 450 prophets (1 Kings 18:18-40). It was there that fire streaking from the clouds burnt up a sacrificial carcass that was drenched in pools of water – making it clear to a terrified nation who God was. The second was the spot at the River Jordan where the waters stopped for the Ark carrying God's Covenant and the children of Israel as they crossed to Jericho (Joshua 3:1-17). In the distance – from where we were – the site of Rachel's Tomb was pointed out.

We visited many New Testament sites too and as we retraced Jesus' footsteps, His entire story came to life in a new way. These places included Jesus' birthplace in Bethlehem, the Shepherds' Field in Bethlehem where the Angel Gabriel appeared to the shepherds and announced the birth of Jesus; Nazareth where Jesus grew up and studied, and the old baptismal site on River Jordan. Then there was the Capernaum on a hill where the only evidence left of the huge synagogue, are pillars. Close by, we saw the site of Peter's home where Jesus healed Peter's mother-in-law's fever.

Another spiritual site was the Mount of Beatitudes where it is said Jesus delivered his first teaching, the Sermon on the Mount. (Matthew 5:1-12) We then went to the Beatitude

Church nearby before visiting the Sea of Galilee and its surroundings. There, we saw a replica of a wooden boat that was found at the bottom of the Sea of Galilee. It was named 'the Jesus Boat'. We got to sail on a replica.

A small van transported us in several trips to Mount Tabor – the Transfiguration Hill – where we learnt about Jesus' Transfiguration (Matthew 17:1-3). After that, we paid a visit to the beautiful church that was erected to commemorate the Transfiguration. Some of us stopped to pray in the church. We saw the ancient sycamore tree that is known as 'Zacchaeus' tree' (Luke 19:1-10). It is protected by a steel fence.

We saw the wilderness where Jesus was tempted for 40 days and the Mount of Temptation (Matthew 4: 1 – 11). Afterwards, we had lunch at the Temptation Restaurant which is located at the base of the mountain.

Other exciting locations were The Via Dolorosa (the Road to Calvary) and Golgotha (the Place of the Skull), the site of Jesus' crucifixion. At the Garden Tomb, with its 'empty tomb' we were informed that controversy surrounds the location of the 'empty tomb' because some history books place it at a different site. I entered the cave and saw the empty tomb. I was able to clearly relate what I saw to my faith. I saw the 'Bible made flesh,' so to speak.

Another interesting place was Jerusalem, where we got to see the Holocaust Memorial and Museum, the Yad Vashem – a memorial to the over six million Jews and other nationalities who were killed by the Nazis. Among the memorial trees with plaques that were planted in memory of Holocaust survivors, I saw a tree that was labelled: 'Corrie ten Boom, a Dutch woman from Holland'.

During our pilgrimage, I came to understand the

importance of Jerusalem, the home of the three Abrahamic religions; Christianity, Judaism and Islam. I sensed why it is said that Jerusalem has always been the centre of God's Heart.

When I returned home, I could not stop talking about our extraordinary tour. I found myself telling my family and friends about the visit, over and over again. At some point, I realised that my attempts to tell the story, so they could really understand what we experienced, were inadequate. My narration did not satisfy me or my listeners because they sometimes asked questions that I could not answer satisfactorily, given that our tour was only eight days long. The main question that my intrigued listeners often asked was, "But are there any Christians there living among those Jews who rejected and killed Jesus?" I realised, once again, that many people are not well acquainted with the Bible and since I wanted to continue sharing my experience, I decided to write about my visit to the Holy land.

The main reason for writing was that I could reach more people as an agent of God's great story. I also wanted to leave a record of my visit so it can still be read long after I am gone. I often quote the saying, "What is not written did not happen." I thank God that He enabled me, in October 2010, to publish a booklet entitled, *The Narration of Mrs Rhoda Kalema of the Pilgrimage to Israel, 20-28 March 2010, with Christians for Israel International.*

Among the pilgrims was a cameraman who took about 900 photographs on the trip. I used a number of them to illustrate my story. My sources of information were the Bible, my notes and the leaflets and booklets that I obtained from the various sites that we visited.

Reverend Dr John Tweedie, who led our group of pilgrims,

launched the booklet at the Redeemed Church at Makerere, when he and his wife Claire, paid a two-week visit to the Christians for Israel branch in Uganda in October of the same year. I gave a number of copies to my family and friends and the rest were put up for sale. It is my hope that my story will inspire others.

Epilogue

In 1993, my daughter, Gladys Nalubowa, introduced me to *Every Day with Jesus*, a Christian devotional publication that was started in 1965 by Reverend Selwyn Hughes. The beginning of each bi-monthly issue, for many years, featured the poems and words of Susan Lenzkes, an American Bible study leader and author. I have learnt a lot from her words. In the January-February 2008 edition, Susan Lenzkes wrote: "Our journey with Jesus is a pilgrimage for foot soldiers. No buses or trains will speed us along; no jets or planes will span our highway to holiness to the Kingdom of Heaven." I can easily relate her words to my journey on earth, and I believe that many people will too, when they ponder their lives.

Like a foot soldier's life, no one's journey is quick or comfortable. Life is often rough, challenging and painful, but, of course, interspersed with joyous and gratifying moments. The longer the journey, the more challenges and joys. In our short or long lives, our story is being written without us realising it.

I have learnt that God has a plan for each of us, His children, and that He places certain people on the different paths to fulfill His purpose in the lives of others. I still carry with me the values, behaviours and beliefs that were instilled in me by my parents and teachers. The conviction of always being conscious of 'a sense of shame' was often stressed to us, children, by our father at home and at King's College Budo by our teachers including the girls' wardens: Agnes Williams, Betty Head and Mary Jewel; as well as house matrons, Ekiria Nakanyolo, Esuka Mwase, Juliana Namala and Rebecca Waligo. Even now, I am careful not to do anything shameful or discourteous, or something that is 'just not done'. Otherwise, "What will people say?"

I recall a lesson I learnt in December 1947 – towards the end of my three-year commercial course at Budo. The headmaster, Dennis Herbert, was about to leave Budo. His father, Lord Hemingford, had just died. Mr Herbert had succeeded him as 2nd Baron Hemingford. He offered me the opportunity to get some work experience in his office and when I reported for work that first morning, I was late. I have never forgotten how he gave me the look that he gave students when he was disciplining them, or how he sternly asked, "You are not going to be late when you start work soon, will you?" I was embarrassed and since then, punctuality is something that I have observed keenly.

Sir Dennis Herbert died in England on 19th June 1982, at the age of 78. At his memorial service at the Namirembe Cathedral later that month, the president of the Old Budonians Club stated, "Headmasters may come, and headmasters may go, but the footprints left by him will never fade, and we shall always try to tread in them." Having him as a school head from the age of twelve to eighteen was a great privilege.

I also fondly remember my special friends from school, Alice Tabu, Mary Kulubya, Alex Musoke, Phoebe Zake, May Bamutta, Jane Bakaluba, and Beatrice Nsubuga who loved me and enriched my life and with whom I created many happy memories.

Since 1958, I have been involved in working for women's progress and leadership. The women's movement enriched my political, professional and personal life as have my mentors, friends and colleagues across three generations. One of my greatest joys, is that many Ugandan women have attained higher education, political awareness, social and civic leadership at home and internationally. However, in spite of all these achievements, I lament the very high rates of adult illiteracy in my country, especially among women. I pray it will improve in the future.

From the 1950s to the 1970s, there were adult literacy programmes at sub-county community centres in rural areas and at the Extra-Mural Department at Makerere University. These were very useful because after they attended the classes, even parents who had previously never been to school gradually came to appreciate the value of educating their children. It is very sad that today, illiterate parents have to be coerced into sending and keeping their children in school. Since literacy is the main door to development and the mind's liberation, I pray that adult literacy programmes will be revived everywhere in my country.

I shall forever be grateful to God for our parents who provided us with a positive environment as we grew up. God also blessed me with a husband, William Wilberforce Kalema, who dearly loved me and encouraged me to pursue further education and supported me immensely during my studies where I got the skills, knowledge and firm foundation to do more than I had ever envisaged in my life. His love, encouragement and belief in me and the life we had together, have been the mainstay of my adult life up to this day.

William and I were blessed with six children. I have always thanked God for their care and love for me. My surviving children: William, Veronica Nakibule, and Gladys Nalubowa have been a source of comfort and strength and I thank them immensely. They overcame their father's early death, and the death of their siblings and went on to make notable contributions in their chosen fields of endeavour. My grandchildren at their different stages in life, have also given me immense joy.

In all the different situations, the one constant is that as I draw closer to God, He draws nearer to me. The book of James (James 4: 8, NIV) assures: "Come near to God and he will come near to you."

At the end of it all, I am able to appreciate and relate my whole journey to God's affirmation in King David's Psalm 138:8 (NIV) "The Lord will fulfill his purpose for me; your steadfast love, O Lord endures forever – do not forsake the work of my hands."

Bibliography

Avirgan, Tony & Honey, Martha, *War in Uganda* (Dar es Salaam: Tanzania Publishing House, 1982).

Brown, Leslie, *Three Worlds: One Word – Account of a Mission* (London: Rex Collings, 1981).

Brown, Winifred *Marriage, Divorce and Inheritance – The Uganda Council of Women's Movement for Legislative Reform* (Cambridge: African Studies Centre, 1988)

International Commission of Jurists Report, *Violation of Human Rights and the Rule of Law in Uganda* (1974)

Kalema, Rhoda, *The Narration of Mrs Rhoda Kalema of the Pilgrimage to Israel; 20-28 March 2010, with Christians for Israel International.*

Kalema, W. W., *Report of the Commission on Marriage, Divorce and the Status of Women* (Kampala: Government Printer, 1965)

Karugire, Samwiri R., *The Roots of Instability in Uganda* (Kampala; Fountain Publishers, 1996).

MacGregor, G. P., *Budo, the First Sixty Years* (Oxford: Oxford University Press, 1967)

Munger African Library Notes, Issue 67, November 1982, California Institute of Technology

Mutesa II (King of Buganda), *Desecration of My Kingdom* (London, Constable, 1967).

Tripp, Aili Mari, *Women and Politics in Uganda* (Kampala: Fountain Publishers, 2000).

Winnie Byanyima and Richard Mugisha (eds), A *Rising Tide – Uganda Women's Struggle for a Public Voice 1940-2004* (Kampala: FOWODE, 2003)

Glossary

Baganda — People of Buganda Kingdom

Balokole — Born-again Christians – followers of a Christian reform movement that began in the 1930s, commonly referred to as "Born Again Christians" or *'Abalokole Abazukuffu'*

Batebe — Prime sister of the Omukama of Bunyore

Buganda — Kingdom in Central Uganda

Bulange — Buganda Houses of Parliament

Bulungibwansi — Communal labour in Buganda

Busuti — (Also known as gomesi) women's dress with origins in Buganda but now considered national attire

Butikiro — Katikiro's official residence

Ekirago — A woven sisal mat

Gakyali Mabaga — So little done, so much more to do

Gombolola — Subdivision of a county (sub-county)

Jajja — Grandmother or grandfather

Kabaka — King of Buganda

Kamala Byona — The final decision maker

Kanzu — Men's long tunic worn over trousers

Kasiki — Traditional ceremony held at both the boy's and girl's homes on the night before the wedding

Katikiro — Official title of the Prime Minister of the Kingdom of Buganda

Kiganda	-	Custom or object of the Baganda people
Kwanjula	-	Traditional pre-wedding ceremony where the bride-to-be introduces her future husband to her parents and relatives; it is considered the most important celebration of the marriage ceremony in Buganda
Lubiri	-	Royal compound or enclosure (Kabaka's palace)
Lubuga	-	Prime sister of the Kabaka of Buganda
Luganda	-	Language of Baganda people
Lukiiko	-	Parliament of Buganda
Lumonde	-	Sweet potato
Lusuku	-	Banana plantation
Maama	-	Mother/mum
Matoke	-	Green bananas and staple food of the Baganda. Also known as matooke
Mengo	-	Capital of Buganda Kingdom
Mpologoma(clan)	-	Clan of Buganda named after a lion
Muganda	-	Person from Buganda
Mulamuzi	-	Chief Justice of the Kingdom of Buganda
Mukulu w'olubiri	-	Head/overseer of the Kabaka's palace (Lubiri)
Mukyala	-	Madam or lady
Muluka	-	Parish
Muwanika	-	Treasurer of the Kingdom of Buganda
Nakyemalira	-	Dictator
Nalinnya	-	Princess of Buganda who is the Kabaka's sister

Namasole	-	Queen Mother in Buganda Kingdom
Nvuma (clan)	-	Clan of Buganda named after a rare underwater plant native to Lake Victoria
Omulangira	-	Prince of Buganda
Omumbejja	-	Princess of Buganda
Rubuga	-	Princess Royal of Tooro
Sabaganzi	-	A person who is full of love
Saza	-	County
Sekiboobo	-	Title for the county chief of Kyagwe
Senga	-	Paternal aunt
Taata	-	Father/dad
Twekobe	-	Kabaka's official house in the palace enclosure

Index

A

Abalokole 43
Aberdeen University 63
Aciro, Rita x
Action for Development (ACFODE) 217, 218
Afro-Asian tournament 99
Ahmad, Maherah 76
Akanga, Byaruhanga 162
Alex Driving School 71
Aligaweesa, Milicent 226
Aliker, Martin 128
Alliance High School 125
American Constitution 196
Amin, President Idi 84, 96, 104, 105, 106, 111, 118, 135, 136, 140, 141, 216
Anglican Church 10, 15, 43, 61, 231, 241, 242
Anglican Consultative Council 135
Anglican Mothers' Union 78
Anglo American Corporation 128
Ankole 9, 96
apartheid 52, 62
Apolo Hotel 159, 167
Arain, Shafiq 110
arrests 158, 164, 165, 166, 176
Arthur's Seat 64
Atlanta 70, 183, 184, 185

B

Bagalaliwo, Sarah 227
Bagenda, Anna 80

Bajabayira, Francis 213
Bakulumpagi, Aloysious 149
Bamusuta 48
Bamusuta Primary School 40
Bamusuta Secondary School 206, 234
Barbour, Reverend Robin 60
Barclays Bank 130, 131
Barnham, Julia 42
Bataringaya, Basil 120
battalion 139, 175
Battle of Lukaya 139
Beijing Conference 216
Bhatia, Hemantini 76
Bible xiii, 50, 61, 103, 129, 167, 179, 184, 231, 232, 233, 236, 238, 242, 243, 244, 245
Bible House 232, 233
Bible Society 230, 231, 233, 237
Bidandi Ssali, Jaberi 149, 162, 213
Bigirwa, Jocelyn x
Bigirwenkya, Flora 94
Bigirwenkya, Zerubabel 168
Bijl, Andrew van der 232, 233
Binaisa, President Godfrey 142, 146, 147
Biraro, Benon 205
Biriba, Dalison 50
Bisiika Primary School 225
Boase, Alice 87
Bright, Bill 185
British 9, 10, 17, 24, 28, 35, 60, 62, 66, 85, 87, 88, 91, 94, 95
British Resident 30

Wycliffe, John xiv